The Williamston
Freedom Movement

The Williamston Freedom Movement

A North Carolina Town's Struggle for Civil Rights, 1957–1970

AMANDA HILLIARD SMITH

McFarland & Company, Inc., Publishers

Jefferson, North Carolina

Library of Congress Cataloguing-in-Publication Data

Smith, Amanda Hilliard, 1983–
    The Williamston freedom movement : a North Carolina town's struggle for civil rights, 1957–1970 / Amanda Hilliard Smith.
        p.   cm.
    Includes bibliographical references and index.

    ISBN 978-0-7864-7636-7 (softcover : acid free paper) ∞
    ISBN 978-1-4766-1433-5 (ebook)

    1. African Americans—North Carolina—Williamston—History—20th century.   2. African Americans—North Carolina—Williamston—Biography.   3. African Americans—North Carolina—Williamston—Interviews.   4. Civil rights movements—North Carolina—Williamston—History—20th century.   5. Williamston (N.C.)—Race relations—History—20th century.   I. Title.
    F264.W684S65 2014
    323.1196'0730756450904—dc23   2014016957

British Library cataloguing data are available

On the cover: *inset* Ella Mae Ormond (left) comforts Jackie Bond during the March on Washington on August 28, 1963 (printed by permission from photographer John Kouns); Sarah Small and Floyd McKissick, CORE national chairmen, lead civil rights protestors to the site of the Voice of America transmitter outside of Williamston. Reprinted from *The Daily Reflector*, December 16, 1963 (© East Carolina University); *background* Eastern North Carolina map (Library of Congress)

Printed in the United States of America

McFarland & Company, Inc., Publishers
    Box 611, Jefferson, North Carolina 28640
        www.mcfarlandpub.com

To my mother,
Nita Hilliard Smith,
my editor and one of my biggest supporters

Table of Contents

Table of Contents

Preface

On July 7, 2011, a North Carolina highway marker was dedicated to the Williamston Freedom Movement. Standing outside of Green Memorial Church of Christ, I could not help but reflect on the journey that had brought me and the other people in the crowd to that moment. When I began my research several years earlier, I had no idea what I would find as I began to investigate my hometown's civil rights movement.

Most people would have a hard time locating Williamston on a map. Its rural location as the county seat of Martin County in eastern North Carolina helps maintain its obscurity today much like it did during the civil rights movements. Fifty years later, the area is still one of the poorest in the state. In the 1960s white business owners only hired whites for the better-paying jobs. If a black person wanted a job that did not involve physical labor, he would have to leave. Willis Williams described the top graduates from E.J. Hayes High School, one of only three black high schools in the county, boarding a bus after graduation and going in search of better opportunities in urban areas.[1] The economic realities of Williamston make the accomplishments of Golden Frinks, Sarah Small, and the other participants in the movement even more impressive.

The more research I did on the Williamston Freedom Movement, the more I discovered how little information was actually written down. Most of the history is documented in newspaper articles and television coverage. Historian Adam Fairclough wrote in *To Redeem the Soul of America* that "news media helps structure reality."[2] With only a few traditional resources available, I found my best resources were oral histories. I have spent hours talking with black and white members of the community about their memories. The voices of Willis Williams,

Joseph Thigpen, George Corey, and many others brought the past alive in a way that school board minutes cannot. I came to see the complexities of the situation and I began to understand how the past affects the present.

I got my first teaching job at Roanoke High School in Robersonville, which is also in Martin County, in 2006. Roanoke was known as the black high school despite desegregation. Most of my students lived in poverty and had been told that their school was the "dumping ground" for students that the other three high schools did not want to teach. I took it as a personal challenge to teach these students about their past. They were inspired to learn that people they had grown up around had achieved amazing things. I brought in people like Styron Bond, Jr., and Francis King, who talked with the students about their participation in the local movement. I encouraged dialogue by bringing in former superintendent Gene Rogers and E.J. Hayes science teacher Clarence Biggs to share their perspectives. It did not take long for my students to come to realize that they, too, could make a difference.

As I encouraged my students to go out and interview their relatives and neighbors, my understanding of the movement increased. I tracked down people whose participation in it led them to leave Williamston, like Alma and Bob Purvis. I traveled to Martha's Vineyard to see their marker to the movement and to meet with people like the Rev. Paul Chapman who had been willing to risk so much to help. I learned from these conversations that the participants had to make fast decisions and adapt quickly to the changing needs of the movement. However, as I went about my research, I did come to some conclusions about the type of strategies that were used. Several factors prevented Williamston from reaching the level of violence and national attention seen in other local movements like Birmingham and Selma.

The non-violent protest technique is a balancing act. The Williamston Freedom Movement needed the counter-protestors to respond with violence to generate attention, but they also wanted to keep their participants from getting killed in a confrontation. When outside newspapers like the *Vineyard Gazette* from Martha's Vineyard and the *Chapel Hill Weekly* began in-depth coverage of the movement, the safety of the participants was increased. The white leadership realized that violence would only bring more attention to the movement and avoided media attention by keeping violence from breaking out in front of reporters.

The law enforcement agencies in Martin County were critical in reducing violence in the movement; they upheld the law, despite their personal beliefs about integration. During one incident, a resident brought a rifle in his car to a march. He told the sheriff that he planned to shoot one of the protestors, and Sheriff Raymond Rawls responded that he was going to have to shoot around him.[3] With protection from law enforcement, the protestors did not experience the kind of violence seen in other parts of the country.

The Massachusetts Unit of the Southern Christian Leadership Conference (SCLC) chose to participate in the Williamston Freedom Movement to increase the reaction of the counter-protestors. According to Golden Frinks, "I told the whites, if you don't talk to us I'll get my friends from the North to come down and we will march white and colored, and it will embarrass you."[4] The presence of white ministers marching with black protestors was particularly upsetting for people in the white community who were worried about race mixing. The choice to send five white women from Martha's Vineyard was also deliberate. The SCLC knew that Southern white men saw themselves as the protectors of white women. The white supporters of the Civil Rights Movement succeeded in increasing the violent reactions of the white community. However, just as more outside news media was beginning to focus on Williamston in November 1963, the assassination of President John F. Kennedy took the spotlight away.

The presence of white supporters of the Civil Rights Movement in Williamston brought it to the attention of people outside the area. One of the women from Martha's Vineyard told a reporter, "They have gained very little so far. They are still wholly segregated, and they still get beaten up. But the focusing of public attention has been helpful, and there has been a great change in their own feelings about themselves."[5] Many of the participants in the Williamston Freedom Movement formed friendships with people from Massachusetts and got the chance to travel outside the state. With their options in Williamston decreasing because of their involvement in the movement, several participants moved in search of better education and job opportunities. As they left, they continued their activism, but the civil rights efforts in Williamston suffered from a lack of leadership.

Most of the participants in the Williamston Freedom Movement were young black women. The movement challenged the traditional male, middle-class leadership in the black community. "Women were going out with only a few men," recalled Ruth Mobley Spruill. "They had to have faith." The non-violent approach was based in the church. However, not all the people who participated in the demonstrations believed in non-violence. This strategy was particularly hard for men to follow, because of traditional ideas of masculinity.[6] The divide within the black community on how the movement should be carried out weakened the efforts of the Williamston Freedom Movement.

Many people in the white community of Williamston were moderate in their approach toward the Civil Rights Movement. Leaders like Mayor N.C. Green and the Rev. Bill Campbell supported the idea of civil rights but felt that the movement was going too fast. They were careful to use means within the law to delay meeting the movement's demands. Eventually the federal government ended segregation in Williamston through the Civil Rights Act of 1964, and the enforcement of the 1954 Supreme Court decision in *Brown v. Board of Education*. It used its outsider position to force an action that many people in the community silently supported.[7] It is easy to forget sometimes that the most vocal people don't necessarily represent the majority.

Civil rights organizations like the SCLC needed media coverage to showcase the hypocrisy of segregation to the rest of the country. The SCLC carefully selected cities where they could send in Martin Luther King, Jr., to set a national goal such as passing voting rights legislation. While the SCLC leadership discussed targeting Williamston, they ended up choosing Selma, Alabama, because of the higher levels of violent resistance and legal repression.[8] The result is that Selma is remembered and Williamston has mostly been forgotten.

In the end Selma is synonymous with violent race relations, while Williamston is only an historical footnote in the Civil Rights Movement. Through understanding the factors that influenced the Williamston Movement, like a rural location that limited resources, law enforcement upholding the law, the lack of national media coverage, the divide in the black community over the strategy that should be used, and the moderate approach taken by the white leadership, it is possible to understand why Williamston never became a major movement.

Timeline

August 9, 1957: An incident between the white Moore family and the black Biggs family results in the death of Rellie Ann Biggs and severe injuries to James Perry Biggs.

September 7, 1957: Joe Cross, a promising A&T student, dies suspiciously after being targeted by the sheriff for harassing a white woman.

1959: Golden Frinks becomes a nationally recognized civil rights activist after leading a protest in Edenton, N.C., over segregation.

April 15, 1963: The "Back Our Brother" campaign increases the number of black registered voters in the county in an effort to get a white man re-elected to town council.

June 1963: Golden Frinks, now a field secretary for the SCLC, is chosen to help lead the Williamston Freedom Movement.

June 30, 1963: Golden Frinks and Sarah Small lead the first protest march to town hall.

July 1, 1963: A protest to desegregate Watts Theatre results in the first arrests.

July 3, 1963: Several young people participate in a sit-in at Griffin's Quick Lunch.

July 4, 1963: A sit-in at Shamrock Restaurant results in Mary Mobley joining the movement.

July 11, 1963: During a march to protest the segregation of S&V Food Store, several marchers are sprayed by an insecticide truck.

July 29, 1963: The KKK burns a 94-foot cross in a field outside of Williamston. It is the biggest burned cross in state history.

July 30, 1963: The police block the protestors' path to town hall, resulting in a 12-hour standoff.

July 31, 1963: The governor stations 72 National Guard troops in

Williamston. Violence is avoided when the mayor agrees to establish a biracial community relations committee.

August 5, 1963: The Williamston Freedom Movement releases "Points of Progress Towards a Free Williamston," which outlines their demands to desegregate public facilities. The same day the town passes an anti-parade ordinance.

August 10, 1963: The Williamston Freedom Movement marches for the first time without a parade permit, and several protestors are placed in jail.

August 28, 1963: Two buses of Williamston protestors participate in the March on Washington.

August 30, 1963: During school registration at E.J. Hayes, students walk out of the school auditorium. When the police block the students' path to town hall, violence erupts near Styron Bond, Jr.'s, store. A few days later shots are fired into the Bond's store.

September 1963: Students at E.J. Hayes boycott over unequal resources.

October 17–18, 1963: Protest outside of the post office results in several injuries.

November 12, 1963: The arrival of 15 white ministers from the Massachusetts SCLC brings publicity to the Williamston Freedom Movement.

November 14, 1963: The first interracial march to town hall results in the desegregation of the county jail.

November 22, 1963: JFK's assassination leads to a temporary break in protests.

December 26, 1963: The Freedom Choir visits the Massachusetts SCLC ministers' churches on a fundraising tour.

February 1964: Frinks is released from jail and embarks on a fundraising trip in the North.

April 1964: During the week before Easter, thirty ministers return to Williamston. The ministers face harassment and several are attacked leaving the Episcopal Church on Easter Sunday.

May 1964: Five Martha's Vineyard women visit Williamston to bring supplies but end up getting arrested for protesting.

Summer 1964: Several black students spend the summer in the North. One of the student leaders, Ralph Hargett, is arrested for stealing a car.

July 1964: The Civil Rights Act becomes law.

July 4, 1964: Reporters from *The Chapel Hill Weekly* and *Vineyard Gazette* spend a week investigating the Williamston Freedom Movement, resulting in an investigative series.

July 1964: Several members of the Freedom Movement travel to St. Augustine, Florida, to participate in the Civil Rights Movement there.

September 1964: Freedom of Choice starts in Martin County schools: twelve black students attend formerly all white schools.

Summer 1965: The Williamston Freedom Movement focuses on voter registration with the help of five white college students from the N.C. Fund.

September 1965: One hundred and five black students transfer schools and teachers start crossing racial lines.

April 4, 1968: Williamston holds a peaceful demonstration after MLK's assassination.

Spring 1968: Sarah Small runs for Congress in the First District. She is joined by five other black candidates running in local elections.

May 1968: Williamston High School changes its qualifications for valedictorian the same year that James Smith, a black student, earns the title.

September 1968: Students at E.J. Hayes boycott over unfair treatment in the desegregation process.

January 29, 1969: Martin County loses federal funds for failure to desegregate.

Fall 1969: The E.J. Hayes football team wins the state championship under coach Herman Boone.

September 1970: Martin County schools desegregate by pairing black and white schools.

People and Events

Chapter One

Joe Cross

Willis Williams was one of the last people to see Joseph "Joe" Cross alive. On September 7, 1957, Williams was waiting outside his family's house for Cross to pick up his older brother, Charlie. The two were planning to drive to Greensboro for their junior year at North Carolina Agricultural and Technical College. Williams, at 15 years old, was responsible for restraining the family's dog when visitors arrived at their isolated home on Barber's Island a few miles outside of Williamston.

It was just beginning to get dark when Williams noticed a cloud of dust on the horizon. Williams first realized that something was wrong by the speed of the approaching cars. When Cross' 1954 Pontiac came to a stop in front of the house, Williams saw one deputy pull Cross out of his car and put him in the back of the sheriff's car. Another deputy drove away in Cross' car. Williams ran inside to report what he had seen to his brother and father. The family did not have a phone so all they could do was wait until the morning to find out what happened to their friend.[1]

The next day Sheriff Raymond Rawls told Cross' stepfather, Jesse Rogers, a very different version of events leading up to Cross' death. A month before, Polly Roberson, a pretty white waitress who worked at the restaurant in the Breezewood Hotel in Williamston, reported to the sheriff that a black man had harassed her. Roberson told the sheriff that he had been driving by her house at night, and that she had received threatening phone calls. She decided to report the harassment after her car windows were smashed twice outside her home.

The sheriff told Cross' stepfather that he decided to set a trap. He had Polly Roberson arrange to meet the caller after she got off work around 9:30 p.m. The sheriff ordered his deputies to station themselves along Highway 64 on the route toward Barber's Island. Then, with a walkie-talkie so that he could communicate with his deputies, the sheriff hid in the back seat of Roberson's car, Deputy Dallas Holliday crouched in the front floorboard, and Roberson drove toward Barber's Island. A motorist in a 1954 Pontiac blinked his lights three times, the agreed-upon signal, and Roberson followed him off the highway into a deserted area known as Lover's Lane.

At the desolate meeting place near Swamp Bridge, an unidentified black man got out of the Pontiac, which Roberson recognized as belonging to her stalker. According to the sheriff's report, Holliday jumped out of Roberson's car and yelled, "This is Deputy Sheriff Holliday; hold it and consider yourself under arrest!" The sheriff tripped over his walkie-talkie, so he was delayed in getting out of the back seat. The black man knocked the flashlight out of the deputy's hands and a struggle took place. Both fell into the front seat of the Pontiac and two shots rang out. The black man was able to get loose from the deputy long enough to drive his car down an embankment into the river. The man, later identified as Joe Cross from his license plate, was rushed to the hospital in a deputy's car but died before he arrived. When Cross' Pontiac was searched, the sheriff found a box of matches, $1.06 in change, some personal papers, and a box of condoms.[2]

When Sheriff Rawls arrived home at 3 a.m., he decided to take his bloody clothes off outside on his porch so as not to alarm his wife. According to the sheriff, his wife shouted a warning that there was a black man holding a rifle in their garden. The sheriff was able to dive behind his car before three bullets were fired at him. The sheriff, along with two police officers, who had just arrived to talk with him about Cross' death, chased the man but were not able to capture him. The sheriff later told reporters that he knew the man's identity, but the man had left town before he could be arrested. The sheriff also claimed that a group of black men had met at a local café after they heard about Cross' death, to "draw straws" to see who would kill the sheriff, believing that it had been the sheriff and not Deputy Holliday who shot Cross.

Joe Cross' body was sent to the coroner, W.W. Biggs, to be examined. The coroner's report stated that "one of the .38 caliber bullets entered the man's right arm at an angle and continued into the body just below the shoulder." A later autopsy reveled that the bullet travelled through the right lung and the aorta before penetrating the left lung. The second bullet was never found. Cross also had a cut across his nose and finger, which could have resulted from the struggle with Deputy Holliday. Cross' knife was found at the scene, which allowed Deputy Holliday to plead self-defense.

Sheriff Rawls was interviewed a couple of times about the Joe Cross case years later. In 1964, he told newspaper reporters that he did not fall getting out of the car but was right behind Deputy Holliday. He claimed to have seen Cross pull a knife on Holliday and said Holliday responded in self-defense by shooting Cross in the right arm. In 1994, Rawls told an oral history interviewer that a scuffle took place between Holliday and Cross, during which Cross pulled a knife. A shootout followed and Cross missed.[3]

The black community was not satisfied with the sheriff's version of events. Cross was a college student and a respected member of the community. It was pointed out that it was unlikely that Cross had been driving in front of Roberson's house, since he had not been in town all summer. He had been working in Norfolk, Virginia, as a carpenter to make money for his family. Cross' stepfather hired a team of lawyers.

Rumors circulated in the black community that Joe Cross had been castrated. The black community was particularly suspicious because Cross' body had been sent to the white funeral home for embalming before it was turned over to the black funeral home for burial. Cross' stepfather exhumed the body twelve days after the burial and had an autopsy performed by a pathologist in Chapel Hill. The expert, Dr. William Forrest, concluded that Cross had not been castrated and that the rumors came from incisions made for embalming.[4] Despite the fact that Cross had not been castrated, the presence of such rumors suggests that most blacks had no trouble believing that the local whites were capable of such an action.

Jet magazine, which famously printed an article on Emmett Till's death two years earlier, covered Cross' death in hopes of creating a similar national outcry over a black man being killed for flirting with a white woman. The article suggested that Cross' murder was a case of mistaken identity. Another black man, Emmett Thomas, who worked as a cook at the same hotel restaurant as Roberson, owned a 1954 Pontiac.

Thomas sold it a few days after Cross' death; he claimed that he was experiencing financial troubles.[5]

Deputy Holliday was indicted on charges of second-degree murder and released on a $7,500 bond. Willis Williams signed an affidavit testifying to what he saw that night. Williams was the one witness who could testify to a different version of events from the sheriff's report. The district attorney offered to let Williams stay in the county jail for protection, but his father refused. The prosecutor never called Williams to testify. The Williams family was told that, at 15 years old, Willis was too young and that his seeing Cross being chased into the family's yard was just a figment of his imagination. With the tracks left by the deputy cars erased the next day by the county's road equipment, there was no physical evidence to back up Williams' testimony. The prosecution only called three of its thirteen witnesses; the defense called no witnesses. After deliberating for fifteen minutes, the all-white jury acquitted the deputy.[6]

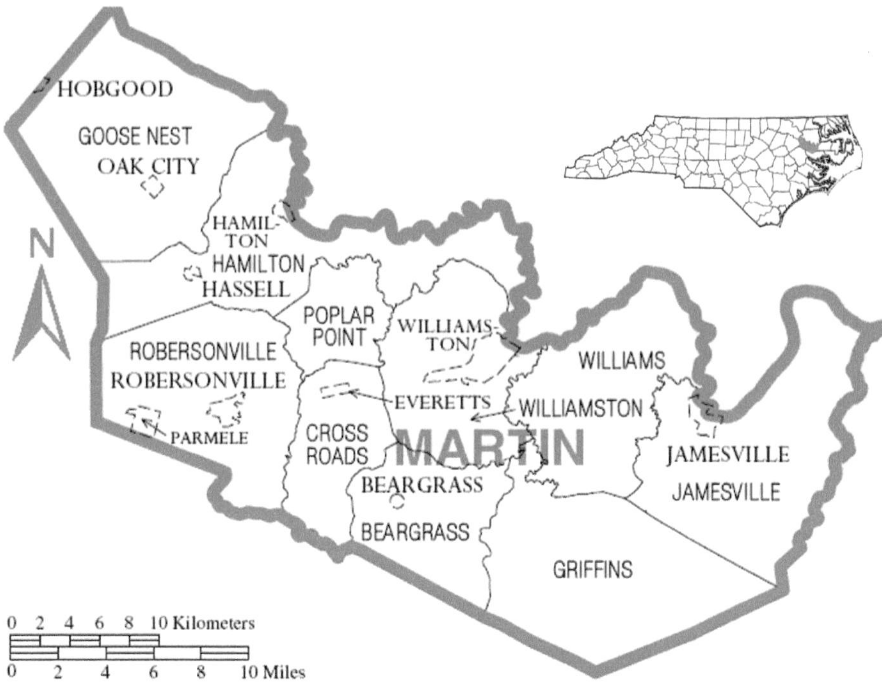

Martin County, northeastern North Carolina.

A Small Town

Williamston is a rural farming community located in the sparsely populated northeastern section of North Carolina. Blacks make up a large percentage of the population from the Tidewater of Virginia to the Mississippi Delta in a region traditionally called the black belt. According to the 1960 census of the 7,000 people who lived in Williamston, 52 percent of the population was white and 48 percent was black.[7] As the chart below

Martin County, North Carolina
1960 Population Distribution
By Age Group, Race, and Sex

Age Group	White Male	White Female	Nonwhite Male	Nonwhite Female	Total 1960	Total 1950
Under 5 years	696	671	1,021	1,001	3,389	4,022
5 - 9 years	697	689	1,099	1,100	3,585	3,557
10 - 14 years	776	706	1,033	1,041	3,556	3,366
15 - 19 years	613	560	711	721	2,605	2,711
20 - 24 years	371	413	311	372	1,467	2,148
25 - 29 years	390	391	287	323	1,391	2,029
30 - 34 years	399	452	286	381	1,518	1,824
35 - 39 years	473	469	328	404	1,674	1,864
40 - 44 years	447	485	331	363	1,626	1,468
45 - 49 years	465	490	322	308	1,585	1,194
50 - 54 years	405	382	250	241	1,278	1,027
55 - 59 years	284	329	183	193	989	798
60 - 64 years	282	256	119	156	813	627
65 years and over	440	548	323	352	1,663	1,303
Total	6,738	6,841	6,604	6,956	27,139	27,938

13,579   13,560

27,139

Age Group	White Male	White Female	Nonwhite Male	Nonwhite Female	Total 1960	Total 1950
Median Age	27.8	29.9	16.0	17.3	21.5	20.7

1960 population distributed by age, race, and sex.

shows, the percentage of white and black citizens was even closer in Martin County. Studies have found that the larger the percentage of blacks, the more the white population fought desegregation.[8] Segregation helped the whites maintain power, which produced economic inequality in the community.

Most of the adult males in Williamston were employed in agriculture, either working in tobacco or peanuts. The white population controlled most of the businesses and wealth. In 1960, the white population owned real property valued at $13 million, while blacks owned only $1.2 million. This means that blacks owned less than one-tenth the wealth compared to their white neighbors.[9] With the black population in a lower social class than the white population, the white population was less likely to accept integration because they did not feel they had anything to gain from it.

The opening of a bus terminal in Williamston with a whites only entrance (courtesy Manning Room, Martin County Community College).

Working-class whites in particular feared that integration would threaten their social and economic status, leading many to believe that blacks were content with their current situation. Once blacks started protesting for their civil rights, many whites had a hard time understanding why blacks were not happy with the status quo. Many whites

A woman and children stand outside of a house in Williamston (Department of Conservation and Development, courtesy John Brooks).

came to the conclusion that the Civil Rights Movement was caused by outside troublemakers and not the local blacks they employed as their maids, handymen, or farm hands. As long as anyone could remember, segregation had been a way of life.

Things began changing across the South in the 1950s as large agri-

A woman and child at a stove (Department of Conservation and Development, courtesy John Brooks).

businesses replaced small family farms. The federal government gave far more support to Southern white planters than to working-class farmers black and white, forcing many families into towns and cities in search of jobs. In Williamston, the number of black citizens living in town increased, which meant a larger base of support for the Civil Rights Movement. However, since most of the better-paying and non-labor intensive jobs in the town were generally available only to whites, there were only a few middle-class blacks, among them school teachers, ministers, and business owners. Very few blacks were economically independent of whites.[10] This meant that a large portion of them had to answer to a white employer for their actions.

A month before Joe Cross' death, an incident between white and black tobacco tenant farmers a few miles outside Williamston demonstrated the inherent problems of blacks being economically dependent on whites. There was a long-standing dispute between the white Moore family who believed that the black Biggs family owed them money for some used clothes. Until the disagreement was settled, Mrs. Rellie Ann Biggs refused to work as a day laborer on the Moores' farm. Mrs. Biggs' refusal would have been viewed as an act of defiance by the Moore family and the rest of the white community.

On the morning of August 9, 1957, the Moore and Biggs children got in a fight over a mule and began throwing rocks at each other. When Mrs. Biggs went to talk with Mrs. Moore about the children's behavior, they got into an argument. Afterward, Mrs. Biggs went to town and swore out an arrest warrant for Mr. L.C. Moore, who she claimed threatened to beat her. A black woman pressing charges against a white man would have been unthinkable.

That evening, when James Perry Biggs arrived home, he drove over to the Moores' house. A few hours later, Mr. Moore called Sheriff Rawls to tell him that he had shot two people. When the sheriff arrived, he found Mrs. Biggs dead from a gunshot wound with her husband lying unconscious on top of a .22 rifle beside her. When Mr. Biggs woke up at Duke Hospital, he was blind, and he could not remember what happened.

Mr. Moore claimed that he shot Mr. and Mrs. Biggs in self-defense. In his statement to the sheriff, he said that he was inside his tobacco

A boy eating beside a stove (Department of Conservation and Development, courtesy John Brooks).

barn when he heard a commotion outside. When he went to investigate, he saw Mrs. Biggs beating his wife with a hoe. Mr. Biggs threatened him, and he shot both Mr. and Mrs. Biggs. The evidence showed Mr. Moore's shot went up the stock of Mr. Biggs' rifle, tore off his little finger and blinded him.

The trial lasted two days. Mr. Moore admitted he had told another man "he planned to kill [Mr. and Mrs.] Biggs." A demonstration broke out in the spectator section of the Martin County Courthouse during Judge Joe Parker's two-hour-long instructions to the all-white jury. The protestors were removed so that when the jury finished deliberating about an hour later, there was hardly anyone in the audience to hear the not guilty verdict.[11]

When both Holliday and Moore were found not guilty of murder,

Above and opposite: Elveta Outterbridge inside Green Memorial Church of Christ (Department of Conservation and Development, courtesy John Brooks).

the black community was reminded of their vulnerability. The town leaders must have sensed their anger because they quickly hired Brad Bagley as the first black policeman in Williamston. However, Bagley did not have the power to arrest white citizens. His presence on the force was symbolic. It would take six years and a series of civil rights protests before Bagley would be permitted to arrest white citizens, which was one of the demands made by the Williamston Freedom Movement in their effort to gain equal rights.[12]

Sarah Small

Sarah Small was a deeply religious woman and gifted pianist who spent most Sundays "making the rounds" as she played at various churches. In the spring of 1963, she returned home from a prayer meeting to find a piece of paper on her front porch advertising a voter registration meeting the next day at Cornerstone Baptist Church. She attended with her brother, J.D. Everett, even though they both were already registered voters. Everett was a member of the National Association for the Advancement of Colored People (NAACP) that met occasionally in Williamston. Everett owned the black funeral home and had seen Joe Cross' body; he knew firsthand that Martin County was not safe for blacks as long as they had no political power.[1]

The meeting at Cornerstone Baptist Church marked the beginning of the "Back Our Brother" campaign. The brother was Thurman Perry, a young white man who had been elected to the town council in 1961 with the support of black voters. Perry had succeeded in getting the trash picked up in the black section of town twice a week after years of complaints about the infrequent garbage collection in their neighborhoods. In an effort to re-elect Perry to the town council, some in the black community had organized a voter registration drive to increase the number of black voters in time for the April 15, 1963, Democratic primary. Since the vast majority of residents in Martin County were registered Democrats, it was the only election that really mattered. The Williamston newspaper, *The Enterprise,* reported that of the 116 new registered voters, 103 were black. On election day the black community made up 20 to 25 percent of the voters, resulting in a record breaking turnout and Perry's re-election.

The number of new black voters was reported with alarm in the newspaper. The black community in Martin County had been relatively successful, compared to other Southern counties, in registering voters through regular registration drives. Two out of every five qualified black voters had succeeded in registering in the county. However, nine out of ten qualified white voters were registered. The literacy test administrated by white registrars often limited the number of blacks that could register. In the late 1940s, when Mary Mobley, a black woman, attempted to register to vote, a white registrar presented her with a passage and asked her to read the word "cemetery." "He put his finger to it," Mobley recalled later. "I said, right where you ought to be." The registrar responded by adding her name to the voting rolls.[2] The number of blacks registered to vote speaks to the activism among the black population even before the national civil rights organizations became involved in the local movement.

The members of the "Back Our Brother" campaign sent a telegram to Martin Luther King, Jr., asking for representatives from the Southern Christian Leadership Council (SCLC) to help them. Beginning in 1960, the John F. Kennedy administration had helped to establish the Voter Education Project (VEP) to coordinate black registration efforts in the South among the four major civil rights organizations. By 1963, the VEP staff was threatening to withhold funds from the SCLC for its lack of activities in assigned areas, including northeastern North Carolina. As a result, Golden Frinks had been hired as an SCLC field secretary because of his experience working on voting campaigns in the northeastern counties of Bertie, Hertford, Pasquotank, and Chowan. With the pressure to increase voting registration activities from the VEP, it is no wonder King hand delivered the letter from Williamston to Golden Frinks at a fundraising dinner in New York City and asked him to "take care of it."[3]

When Frinks arrived in Williamston in June 1963, he discovered he had competition from a mild-mannered representative from the NAACP. According to Frinks, "I got up there and asked them, do you want your freedom? I jumped all up on tables and everything, really clowning." After Frinks' performance, the Williamston Freedom Movement decided to become affiliated with the SCLC, with Golden Frinks as their representative.[4]

Frinks organized the first meeting at the Rev. David Carter's Bible

Way Church, which was meeting in a tent at the end of Sycamore Street in Williamston. Ida Small Speller, one of Sarah Small's daughters, wrote about her mother asking her and her younger brother, Jimmie, if they would like to march. Speller recalled her excitement thinking that there would be bands and majorettes involved. Instead, when she got to the meeting, she remembers, Frinks was telling the group of 7 to 10 young people about injustices facing blacks and how marching would "turn all of this around." Afterward the Rev. Fred LaGarge from Edenton, who served as the SCLC's regional representative, Frinks' assistant, and the movement's piano player taught the group a few freedom songs, songs that the young people already knew from church but with the words altered to fit the purposes of the Civil Rights Movement.

After church the next day, June 30, the young people participated in the first of many marches to town hall. Speller wrote that, at the time, "none of us really knew exactly what was going to happen or the magnitude of what we were preparing to embark on." Sarah Small, who was down the street visiting with a friend, was not aware of the march until she saw the group pass by the house. She told her friend, Wardell Brown, that she "could not allow some people from another town lead our children." Despite being six weeks pregnant, she walked up to the front of the line. Law enforcement officers diverted traffic so that the marchers could walk down the middle of Main Street. A crowd formed on the sidewalk, but no one stopped the demonstration. At town hall the marchers prayed and sang "We Shall Overcome" before returning to the tent. The next night more young people joined the movement.[5]

It did not take long for the leaders to realize that they were quickly outgrowing the tent. Every church that they approached refused the movement access out of fear that their church would be bombed or burned down. This was not an irrational fear; many black churches throughout the South that hosted civil rights meetings were targeted. Two months later, 16th Street Baptist Church in Birmingham, Alabama, was bombed; four young girls were killed and 23 others attending Sunday school were injured.

Sarah Small had connections to several churches where she played the piano. One Saturday, after playing for a rehearsal for the junior choir at Green Memorial Church of Christ, she approached the head deacon,

The Williamston Unit of the SCLC featured in the 1964 SCLC calendar. Ella Mae Ormond and Sarah Small (front row, left to right), the Reverend Pettaway, unknown, Jackie Bond, Mary Mobley, and Vina Hodges (second row, left to right), two unknown women and John Small (back row, left to right) (courtesy Styron Bond).

William Dorsey Speller, and asked if it was possible for the movement to meet there. Speller convinced the congregation to take the risk. As a result, he became one of the first people to lose his job (he worked at a gas station) due to his connection to the movement.

For the next 32 nights, the Williamston Freedom Movement held meetings at Green Memorial. Alma Freeman Purvis, who grew up attending the church, felt that it made sense that Green Memorial hosted the movement. "Green Memorial was always up for the community. It has always been a church that reached out to help people." She described a family atmosphere in which women like Hattie Speller would cook and perform other duties for the surrounding community referred to as "down the hill."[6]

Green Memorial Church of Christ sits near the dividing line on

Golden Frinks and Sarah Small outside of Green Memorial Church of Christ (photograph by Charles Clark, Department of Conservation and Development, reprinted from Capus Waynick, John Brooks, and Elsie Pitts, *North Carolina and the Negro*, North Carolina Mayors Co-operating Committee [Greensboro, 1964], p. 167, courtesy John Brooks).

Main Street which separated "uptown," where whites controlled business, and "down the hill," where the blacks lived. A few steps are all that divide the street, but the sections could not have been more different in terms of fire hydrants, street signs, and streetlights. The protestors did not set out to end segregation; they simply wanted equal rights and a fair distribution of the town's funds.

At the nightly meetings, participants received information about the movement as well as training in non-violence from their leaders. Ida Small Speller recalled that one night after a non-violence training session at Green Memorial Church of Christ, the door burst open and several male members of the movement came running into the chapel. She described what sounded like gun shots being fired and the men with blood on their heads and arms. It turned out that the leaders had decided to stage the invasion to see how participants would react.[7] The group was shaken, but reminded of the dangers they faced.

The mass meetings built up the participants' courage before a march. Occasionally a minister preached but most nights someone from the movement led the marchers in a prayer. Speeches by Sarah Small or Golden Frinks were accompanied by the Freedom Choir, which was made up of young people from the community. The Reverend LaGarge played the piano; according to some, his style was similar to Jerry Lee Lewis. The freedom songs were sometimes used to pass along a message about an upcoming boycott or the likelihood of the protestors facing jail. Mostly, the music got the protestors ready to face whatever might be waiting for them outside.

"We told people that if they couldn't handle non-violence, then they needed to get out," recalled Francis King. "Before we could leave the building, some of the members, like myself, would take any weapons from the marchers and if anyone was suspected of hiding weapons, we would search them." The fact that some people tried to hide weapons shows that not everyone agreed with the non-violent approach. Some historians have argued that non-violent strategies failed to attract men because it went against traditional ideas of masculinity. Bob Purvis admitted that he and other men in the movement had trouble with the concept of non-violence. It was not uncommon for black men to position themselves within the crowd of counter-protestors to keep them from attacking marchers.

As the congregation left the church, the protestors formed two lines. Sarah Small and Golden Frinks, if he was in town, led the march. The youth leaders, Annette Armstrong Lanier, Alma Freeman Purvis, Jackie Bond Shropshire, William Nelson, Robert Purvis, John Small, Vinnie Hodges, Mary Hansome and Clara Gross, were next. The marchers walked on both sides of the sidewalk to avoid walking in the road as they marched toward town hall. Styron Bond, Jr., 16 years old at the time, recalled an old white woman who sat on her porch combing her silver hair every night. "I would look at her as we passed because I knew that we were not going to be coming back. We would be arrested."[8]

If the marchers reached their destination, they prayed and sang freedom songs, which they had adapted by adding names of local officials. The protestors sang, "Sheriff Rawls ain't gonna turn us around, turn us around, turn us around." Angry crowds of whites gathered nearby threatening violence. When possible, the marchers returned to church after a protest to assess and evaluate their approach. "Without debriefing some of us would have been deeply scared and would have figured out other methods that weren't non-violent," reflected Bob Purvis. "There was constant talk about our purpose and why we were there."

During the summer of 1963, similar civil rights protests were taking place all over the South. Earlier in the spring, Martin Luther King, Jr., was arrested for marching in Birmingham, Alabama. Race riots were taking place in Greensboro, North Carolina; Lexington, North Carolina; and Danville, Virginia. "We were protesting in Williamston the lack of opportunity and rights," recalled Francis King. "It was like something was in the air all over America." King, who at age 26 was one of the older participants in the movement, recalled a generational divide between her and her father. "My dad was from a different generation and could not understand why we were participating. He would say things like 'I do not want to sit beside a white person' and I would say that is not the point." Some older people in the black community did support the movement, but the majority of the participants were young people. They had experienced segregation and were willing to risk everything, even their lives, to change society.

Even people who could not directly participate, like Bob Purvis' mother who worked as a maid for a white family, supported the movement. "People who felt they couldn't do anything sent money or food," said Bob Purvis. "People did the things that the black community had always done when they saw people doing something that was worthwhile." It was Sarah Small's passion for civil rights that inspired others in the local community to rally behind the SCLC and Golden Frinks. "Ms. Sarah's involvement got all of us involved," recalled Bob Purvis. The Smalls' house was across from the house he grew up in. He credited Small's involvement with giving the black community a sense of ownership in the movement.

In black communities where male middle-class teachers, ministers, and professionals had typically been seen as the leadership, a new group of women were taking their place. One morning, Small entered Green Memorial Church of Christ to find an election in progress. "The people were standing up," she remembered. "Somebody says, 'Stand up.' I stood up, too, and they said, 'You've just been voted president.' And I said, 'What?'" Brenda Williams was elected secretary, Hattie Speller assistant secretary, Levester Harris treasurer, and Ella Mae Ormond executive director.[9]

Sarah Small later talked to a reporter about why black men were largely absent from the front lines of the movement. "There were far more black women and their children than black men in the movement then, because in the South the men had typically been targeted more for violent retribution by whites, including beatings, shootings, and lynchings—and they were rightly afraid."[10] Men like Golden Frinks put their lives at risk leading the movement. When NAACP Field Secretary Medgar Evers was killed on June 15, 1963, Frinks made several remarks about his days being numbered, too. He believed that he was constantly in danger because of his civil rights activities. Frinks avoided driving alone, and he was careful never to spend more than two or three days in Williamston at any given time.[11]

Men were also more vulnerable to economic reprisal since they typically earned more money. Even though Sarah Small's husband stayed home to watch the children while she marched, his teaching contract at Swan Quarter in Hyde County was not renewed the next fall because of his wife's civil rights activities. He ended up having to leave for New York to find employment.[12] The black men directly involved in the movement were usually ministers because their livelihood could not be threatened by the white community. Golden Frinks was not a minister, but his employment by the SCLC gave him economic independence.

Golden Frinks

Golden Frinks' personality made him a controversial figure. However, most people, including Frinks himself, said he was the driving force behind the Williamston Freedom Movement. Frinks said, "I'm the sparkplug here. I'm what makes things tick. Without me, if I were to go, all the gains we've made would be gone in a few days." While it is true that Frinks initiated most of the movement's activities, he did receive assistance from dozens of local residents as well as several national organizations, in addition to the SCLC.

In the 1960s Golden Frinks was a trusted advisor to Martin Luther King, Jr., and one of twelve field secretaries for the SCLC. His life experiences had prepared him to be a community organizer in northeastern North Carolina. Frinks was raised in Tarboro, North Carolina. At the age of six, he was sent to live with the white Lewis family as a companion for their little boy. By all accounts, he was treated as an equal, which would have made the discrimination that he encountered later in his life harder to accept.

During World War II, Frinks was stationed in the Persian Gulf where he set up non-commissioned officers' clubs. After the war, he moved to Washington, D.C., and then Edenton, North Carolina, where he established several integrated nightclubs for servicemen. When two mixed couples were arrested at one of his clubs, Frinks was charged with "providing white prostitutes for black Marines" and lost his liquor license.

This experience with racism led Frinks to establish a chapter of the NAACP in Edenton. In 1959, a group of high school-age girls approached the local chapter, frustrated because they were not able to eat ice cream at the drug store where they bought it. Frinks successfully organized the young people of Edenton to produce one of the first civil rights victories in North Carolina.

Golden Frinks, field secretary of the Southern Christian Leadership Conference, in 1964 (Department of Conservation and Development, courtesy John Brooks).

Golden Frinks quickly became one of the most important civil rights organizers in the eastern part of the state, gaining the attention of the SCLC. Frinks proved that "nonviolent direct action" could work in rural, isolated areas. Unlike most civil rights leaders until that time, Frinks drew his local leadership not from the educated middle class but from the working class. Frinks was more in touch with rural blacks than most SCLC leaders who came from large Southern cities.[1] Frinks' experience taught him that rural movements required the building up of trust within the black community.

Alma Freeman Purvis, a young black student involved in the movement, recalled, "People felt like Golden Frinks had your back. He is going to get you a lawyer, get you out of trouble; he is going to be there for you, whatever." Ruth Mobley Spruill agreed. "He would give people the shirt off his back as well as the shirt of anyone who was with him. He was a good man." Frinks' ability to inspire trust was critical to the movement, especially since he needed parents to trust him with their children.

On July 1, 1963, the day after the first march down Williamston's Main Street, Frinks led a group of young people to attempt to desegregate Watts Theatre. It required blacks to sit in the balcony, called "Buzzard's Roost." This insult was made even more apparent during World War II, when German prisoners from the nearby prisoner of war camp were allowed to sit downstairs with the white customers.

Brenda Williams was the first to walk up to the white side of the ticket counter. "The person who sold the tickets denied Williams a ticket, and she wanted to know what made her money any different from a white person's," recalled Ida Small Speller, who was with the group that day. "She said it has 'In God We Trust' on it, and that George Washington was on her dollar too." Frinks told the students that if they were refused a ticket to immediately sit down and block the entrance, which they did. They were arrested for trespassing.

Ida Small Speller was only 13 the first time she was arrested. Speller and others under 16 lied about their ages because law enforcement officers would release them to their parents instead of keeping them in jail. Frinks later told an interviewer, "We had to break their fear. We got the children to understand they had to work together, learn to obey and follow a leader."[2] It was mostly young people who went to jail.

A couple of days after the protestors had gotten out of jail, a group of around 12 young people decided to desegregate Griffin's Quick Lunch, where blacks sat up front and white customers ate in the back dining room. There was only a limited number of seats in the dining room so the protestors had to break into smaller groups. As one group got arrested, another group would take their place until they all were arrested. One of the participants, Styron Bond, Jr., recalled that when a white customer picked up a chair to throw at the protestors the "owner told the man not to hurt us. He said that is what we [the protestors] want them to do." The reaction of the business owner showed that he was aware that the use of violence in other movements had resulted in media attention in favor of the protestors. When the police arrived, one of the officers knew the Bond family and told Styron and his sister Jackie that they did not have to participate since they came from a respected black family. However, the siblings chose to go to jail. Jackie Bond Shropshire lied and said she was 16, not 15, so that the police would keep her in jail instead of releasing her to her parents. According to Styron Bond, Jr., "It was not a punishment when it was what you wanted. It was like getting a notch on the belt every time you went to jail."[3] For some protestors, getting arrested was a way to show their commitment to the movement.

Golden Frinks was a mentor to the young people. He gave the youth leaders a lot of responsibility, but he also made sure that he praised their accomplishments. "He was excellent at building your self-esteem. He saw your gifts and talents," said Alma Freeman Purvis. "He was very respectful and never talked down to us. When we raised concerns, he would listen and take into account what we said." Frinks also understood that the youth leaders needed to have the opportunity to be children. Frinks would occasionally take a group of students out to just enjoy themselves. "We could goof off and have some fun. He felt it was necessary that we have a normal life as well. We got to act like normal kids," said Alma Freeman Purvis.

Once local business owners learned about the Williamston Freedom Movement's efforts at desegregation, many chose to close their doors when they saw protestors approaching. The swimming pool was closed and later turned into a parking lot. The bowling alley was closed temporarily. When protestors tried to integrate Martin General Hospital, the receptionist refused to take their information until they went to the "colored" side. At Leggett's Drug Store, after two different groups requested service at the counter, Paul Leggett took the seats off the stools in front of the soda fountain, forcing white and black customers to stand.[4]

On July 4, 1963, more than 200 blacks led by Sarah Small and Golden Frinks declared their independence by testing desegregation laws in local establishments. One group went to Shamrock Restaurant, where Mary Mobley worked in the kitchen. Mobley, who had received the right to vote by intimidating the white registrar, was not a woman to mess with. When her boss locked the protestors out, Mobley threw down her apron, unlocked the doors, and the entire black staff of the restaurant followed her. According to Mobley, "I knew about the sit-ins up in Greensboro, and I told myself if they ever came here, I was in it." From that day forward, Mobley became an important leader in the Williamston Freedom Movement.

Mary Mobley was known for her bravery. According to her daughter Ruth Mobley Spruill, "Civil rights for her was never about hatred, but about doing what is right. She hated the way people were treated; it was about equality of people. People deserved to be treated equally." One night while the marchers were singing in front of town hall, a sheriff's deputy asked Mobley if she thought she was going to heaven. When she answered in the affirmative, the deputy responded that if she went to heaven he wanted to go to hell. Mobley said, "In hell you'll lift up your eyes to see me." According to her daughters she had no fear. "If she died doing this, then this is what God had intended for her life. She was not going to allow anyone to treat her or anyone's children with disrespect," said Ruth Mobley Spruill.[5]

After ten consecutive nights of marches downtown, 200 protestors returning to Green Memorial on July 9 were assaulted by counter-protestors. Frinks sent a telegram to the governor asking for protection; he claimed "an unruly mob of several hundred jeering whites surrounded the marchers, kicked some of them, burnt some of them with cigarettes and serious violence appeared imminent despite the presence of local police." Chief of Police Lloyd Banks downplayed the incident by claiming that the mob was "between 50 to 75 young boys with no leader who were just shooting off their mouths." He said law enforcement had the situation under control and he did not plan to ask for assistance from the state. Gov. Terry Sanford never commented on the telegram.[6]

Sarah Small spent a lot of time praying before making decisions about the movement. On July 11, 1963, a group of protestors visited S&V

Food Store to see if it would agree to integrate. The owner's son informed the group that "if the local people had come to talk to him first, it would have been different, but since we got those Yankees in town, he would refuse to even permit us on his property." That night, instead of marching to town hall, Sarah Small felt led to march to the supermarket. According to the town, an insecticide truck had stopped in the street in front of the store to avoid hitting a black child. It stalled and accidentally sprayed the protestors with mosquito repellent.[7] The protestors saw the incident differently. Ida Small Speller claims a "light wind came and lifted the fog right over our heads, and no one coughed or got sick." She and others felt that it was divine protection, God's way of showing that He was shielding them from harm.[8]

When members of the movement attempted to desegregate the Martin Memorial Library on August 9, 1963, the librarian locked the doors when she saw them approaching even though there were white patrons inside. Six days later, when the protestors returned to the library, they found a sign saying that the librarian was on vacation. The library had been built with contributions from the all-white Women's Club, but maintained by town funds. Instead of integrating, the library board decided to become private, and the town was forced to stop paying the library's operating and maintenance costs. In a newspaper article, a member of the KKK claimed that the organization was contributing to the library to make up for the loss of town funds.[9] The library remained segregated until the Civil Rights Act of 1964 was passed.

The white community struggled to understand the Williamston Freedom Movement. "When it first began we had demonstrations and marches. That was really unnerving to white people," recalled Marie Robertson. "The togetherness of the black people was something that they were not accustomed to." Alton Hopewell added, "From an outsider's point of view, it was like a carnival scene with the marches taking place every night. We could hear the noise of people clapping, and the marching band from our house."[10]

Many people in the white community felt that Williamston had great race relations before Golden Frinks' arrival and that the town was a victim of being too close to where Frinks lived. Joseph Thigpen, who was vice chairman of the county commissioners, remembered an

Ella Mae Ormond (left) comforts Jackie Bond during the March on Washington, August 28, 1963 (used by permission of photographer John Kouns).

incident in which Frinks showed up to the county commissioners meeting without an appointment. "I physically escorted him out because he wasn't going to interrupt business. I was serious about him not being in the room without an appointment." Many of the town leadership told reporters that Williamston was targeted by Frinks because it had "cordial race relations," that Frinks came to Williamston because he felt he could be successful in achieving his demands.[11]

The white leadership was quick to point out Frinks' various arrests to try to discredit him. Frinks was convicted of writing bad checks, which Frinks always claimed were the result of his involvement with civil rights activities. Frinks explained to a reporter that he kept close tabs on the money used for the movement, but that local merchants held his checks until the end of the month so that his balances were not accu-

All three photographs: **Jackie Bond and Golden Frinks singing at the March on Washington, August 28, 1963 (courtesy Leonard Freed family).**

rate. In addition, his bank stopped notifying him when his account was overdrawn. It became a common sentiment among the white community that Frinks' "biggest accomplishment in town was writing bad checks."[12]

In the black community, Frinks' record did not stop him from raising money. Bob Purvis remembers driving Frinks to black-owned businesses, particularly nightclubs, and always leaving with money. "He made sure they understood that their money was being well used for the cause." One of those business owners, Ella Mae Ormond, contributed enough money to provide two buses for members of the movement to attend King's famous "I Have a Dream" speech during the March on Washington on August 28, 1963.[13]

Sarah Small kept Golden Frinks grounded. Frinks was an incredible community organizer, but he would take a lot of chances. "Some people didn't like Frinks' methods. Since it was a black church movement, some people believed in waiting for God. Frinks believed that you had to take a firm stance," said Willis Williams.[14] Whether they approved of Golden Frinks' methods or not, everyone agrees that he played a critical role in the Williamston Freedom Movement.

Chapter Four

Sheriff Raymond Rawls

Sheriff Raymond Rawls was still in office six years after Joe Cross' death. He was first elected sheriff in 1954 and had served on the Williamston Police for several years before that. The sheriff, with two full-time and six part-time deputies, was responsible for maintaining order in the county.[1]

On the night of July 29, 1963, Martin County became the center of Ku Klux Klan activity for northeast North Carolina. The Klan sent a message to the Williamston Freedom Movement by erecting a cross in an unplanted field just outside of the town limits. At 94 feet, it beat a state record set earlier in Wilmington. One unidentified member of the Klan in an interview claimed that "there was no need for the Klan until we got people like Frinks. The white people around here had to have some means of having a voice in local affairs, and it didn't look like the laws and the government were going to protect us, so the Klan started organizing."

According to the same man, the Klan was helping law enforcement keep order in the county. "This is a right big county, and it's too much for three men to take care of. Anything we can do to help him [the sheriff], we're glad to. That's part of our oath. We're sworn to uphold the law and cooperate with any law enforcement agency." There were claims by the Williamston Freedom Movement that the Klan had penetrated law enforcement. Members of the black community complained that the police passed out clubs to the white mobs to attack protestors and that the sheriff had on at least one occasion gone out into the rural areas of the county with a loudspeaker to rally white counter-protestors.[2] It appears that whatever type of relationship law enforcement had with the Klan, someone was able to exercise control over members of the Klan to keep them from directly attacking the marchers.

Tensions were running high the day after the burning of the cross.

Ku Klux Klan cross burning ceremony in a field outside of Williamston, July 29, 1963 (used by permission of *The News & Observer*).

Sheriff Raymond Rawls was first elected sheriff in Martin County in 1954 (courtesy Manning Room, Martin County Community College).

That night Sheriff Rawls and his deputies blocked the marchers' path to town hall at the steps dividing downtown and "down the hill." Sarah Small, now obviously pregnant, was leading the march. The marchers refused to return to Green Memorial Church of Christ, so they just sat down where they stood. Small later told an interviewer, "Finally, everyone on both sides got tired of standing so long and sat down, and some of us got to talking. If we can sit down together out here, why can't we do it inside any of these buildings up and down the street here?"

Law enforcement attempted to break up the marches with cattle prods. Blue Watson, who was a large guy, was struck with a cattle prod several times but did not flinch. The officer then tested it on himself to see if it was working and was almost knocked out. An officer chased Joe Carney Brown down the hill with a billy club. "The harder they hit him the slower he walked," remembered Ida Speller Small. "I didn't know he had that kind of strength in him." Another marcher, Arthur Leary, pulled a pocket knife on one of the counter-protestors. Sheriff Rawls jumped on a car and told the crowd to let him handle it. Leary was arrested but not before members of the Williamston Freedom Movement claimed that he was left mentally impaired from the beating he took. The 12-hour standoff finally ended with a compromise between Small and the sheriff. Small agreed to take the marchers back to the church, if the sheriff agreed to disperse the white counter-protestors.[3]

The next day, 74 National Guard troops were in Williamston on stand-by. Official reports estimated 600 to 700 armed whites gathered downtown waiting for the protestors. "I was told not to go downtown. So of course I went," said Betsy Harrison Conway. "I saw National Guard troops standing arm in arm. I ran into my dad on the way out, and he told me to get on home." According to Sheriff Rawls, "After 32 nights, things here were at a fever pitch. The people out in the county had begun to leave the children at home, put their shotguns in the car and come to town."

A showdown was averted when Gen. Capus Waynick, Gov. Terry Sanford's most senior mediator of local civil rights disputes, convinced Mayor N.C. Green to hold a meeting of the Biracial Community Relations Committee. Frinks agreed to stop demonstrations until they had a chance to negotiate. The marchers went home, thinking that a disaster had been avoided.[4]

The Biracial Community Relations Committee had been established a month earlier in Williamston after Gov. Sanford's meeting with local government officials on the state's racial crisis. At the meeting, the governor stated that he felt federal civil rights laws were a violation of business owners' rights to choose who they serve. To avoid federal intervention, he encouraged local government officials to set an example for the nation by carrying out desegregation in an orderly fashion. Gen.

Waynick told the audience they were "being unrealistic if they think they will avoid the Negro demands." After returning from the meeting, Mayor Green appointed white businessman Russell W. Bondurant chairman of the newly-created Biracial Community Relations Committee. The original committee was made up of five blacks and five whites plus the white mayor and chairman. The committee was later expanded in May 1964 to 10 black and 12 white members, a move that the leaders of the Williamston Freedom Movement claimed was to dilute their votes.

Mayor Green, who was first elected mayor in 1955, was widely praised by the white community for the way he handled the Williamston Freedom Movement. The mayor and the committee's chairman, Russell Bondurant, were both businessmen with reputations as moderates. However, the movement leadership claimed that the men had done a lot to "discredit the movement in certain quarters."

The Williamston Freedom Movement viewed most of the black members of the committee as "Uncle Toms," submissive to the mayor and chairman who appointed them. Sarah Small and Styron Bond, Sr., were the only people on the committee involved in the Williamston Freedom Movement, and Golden Frinks was not permitted to attend meetings because he was viewed as an outsider. Among the black members was Willie Bunch, who owned a barbershop which served white customers only. He told a visiting reporter that the protestors "are scum, troublemakers. They have set young-uns to running by my place, yelling names—Uncle Tom—I have never had any trouble before."[5] The white leaders' idea of "the responsible Negro leadership" came to mean any black person not participating in the Civil Rights Movement.

On August 5, 1963, the Williamston Freedom Movement submitted a list of demands called "Points for Progress Towards a Free Williamston," which focused on integrating public facilities such as schools, the hospital, and businesses. Frinks submitted a similar list of demands to the Bertie County Commissioners on the same day.[6] The committee agreed to remove all signs for separate facilities in government buildings, adopt an employment policy without regard to race for government jobs, to stop listing property taxes by race in the newspaper, and allow the town's only black police officer, Brad Bagley, to arrest white citizens. The committee also prepared a petition asking the school board to desegre-

WHAT WE ARE FIGHTING FOR   WE FIGHT FOR OUR RIGHTS

DEMANDS OF THE WILLIAMSTON UNIT OF SCLC

1. DESEGRATION OF ALL PUBLIC ACCOMODATIONS.

2. DESEGREGATION OF ALL COUNTY AND CITY BUILDINGS

3. USE OF COURTESY TITLES BY PRIVATE BUSINESS AND PUBLIC OFFICIALS.

4. INCREASED POWER OF THE BI-RACIAL COMMISSION.

5. FAIR EMPLOYMENT PRACTICES.

6. REGISTRATION BOOKS OPEN FOR AT LEAST 60 DAYS A YEAR.

7. END OF POLICE BRUTALITY.

8. INTEGRATION OF TAX ROLLS

9. END OF UNJUST ORDINANCES AND INJUNCTIONS.

10. DROPPING ALL CURRENT CHARGES GROWING OUT OF DEMONSTRATIONS.

WHAT WE ARE FIGHTING FOR   WE FIGHT FOR OUR RIGHTS

List of demands released by the Williamston Freedom Movement (David King Papers, Duke University, courtesy SCLC).

gate the public schools.[7] The Williamston Freedom Movement originally viewed the committee's response as a major victory.

However, before the Williamston Freedom Movement could celebrate, the town council met in a closed meeting later that day where they passed an anti-parade ordinance, which made marching without a permit illegal. The anti-parade ordinance required 24-hours' written notice to law enforcement before demonstrations, and it banned people under 18 from marching without special permission. The protestors saw this as "an act of bad faith." Frinks filed an injunction against the anti-parade ordinance in the Superior Court.[8]

Mayor Green claimed that the ordinance was passed before the civil rights marches had started in Williamston. "We, like all other towns, have ordinances regulating demonstrations," said Mayor Green. "We have never enforced them or attempted to enforce them." George Corey, a member of the town council, claimed that the anti-parade ordinance had been passed several months earlier after a strike at the local Texaco oil refinery.[9]

The first few times the leaders of the Williamston Freedom Movement applied, the permit was granted. Ida Small Speller wrote about the first time the group marched after getting the permit:

> On the way up the hill after the steps there were a lot of white jeerers standing on the sidelines. I remember hearing one lady saying, "Daddy get yo gun and shoot the niggas," and he said, "Ah hell, I ain't going to jail for no nigga." Once we all had passed them they followed us to city hall; once we got there we sung a few songs and then we kneeled to pray. I can't remember who prayed that night, but the prayer was so powerful that the power of the Holy Spirit visited everyone out there. When I looked up the lady who had coaxed her daddy to get his gun had her hands up in praise; that was a very powerful night. When we marched back to church, most of the jeerers had left.[10]

The first time the permit was denied, according to Francis King, "it was time to start filling the jails." On August 10, 1963, Sarah Small informed the group that they were going to march without the permit and warned everyone that they might get arrested. Golden Frinks had promised the governor that he would not lead a demonstration until after the anti-parade ordinance had been tried in court; he did say that others would try to march. Ida Small Speller, Sarah Small's daughter, who was then 13, remembers the children being very excited about the prospect of going to jail as part of civil disobedience. That night 54 protestors were arrested for violating the ordinance.

Going to jail put a burden on the family, so it was not something that all participants could do. Francis King chose not to place herself in situations where she would likely get arrested since she had several young children. Alma Freeman Purvis remembers being in jail with her mother and sisters, and her father having to come bail out her mother because there was no one at home to cook supper.[11] Going to jail was a way to show commitment to the movement, but it was not a decision that was made lightly.

At $200 a person, bond was a challenge for most participants in the movement. On several occasions, Styron Bond, Sr., bonded protesters out of jail because he was a business owner who had land to put up as collateral. Court records show that he posted bail for 17 people. According to his son, Styron Bond, Jr., "He ran out [of money] before he got to me. The worst part was seeing the family car leaving the parking lot, and I was not in it." His father was later able to convince John Reddick, an owner of a cab company, to post bail for his son.[12]

Until they posted bail, the protestors were under the care of Roy Peel, who had just been honored for his 30 years of service as jailer. The protestors fondly referred to him as Uncle Roy. His wife cooked for the jail, but he would allow women from "down the hill" like Hattie Mae Speller to send in food. The women sent fried chicken, collard greens, cornbread and desserts until someone finally decided that the protestors were too comfortable in jail. At that point the protestors were limited to the food that the town provided. Protestors said Uncle Roy felt sorry for them because they were forced to eat his wife's cooking.[13]

It was summer and the protestors had quickly filled the jail. According to some reports there were as many as 50 men in cells that were not meant for more then eight. Frinks charged that protestors were "packed like sardines" in cells while a nearby cell for whites was unoccupied. The protestors sang freedom songs and rattled the doors of their cells well into the night. Peel told the protestors they had to be quiet because they were disturbing people living in nearby houses. When they did not stop, the windows in the jail were closed. Some people claimed that the heat was turned on to make the conditions more miserable. John Small believed that water was pooling on the floor from perspiration; the men were dehydrated. Others claimed that the men turned on the water in the sinks and stopped up the drains so they could cool off. When the water reached the ladies' cells, the jailer came to see what was going on and opened the windows.[14] On purpose or not, the conditions in the jail were not pleasant.

From the white perspective, the movement was draining the community's resources as more money had to be spent to pay for the increased demands on law enforcement officers and jails. Sheriff Rawls and Police Chief Lloyd Banks were in a difficult situation because they did not have the resources or experience to handle the daily and nightly protests. They both denied to reporters that the protestors were being mistreated. However, Golden Frinks and Sarah Small filed several complaints against law enforcement for using unnecessary force against protestors.

Martin County Courthouse and Jail (courtesy Manning Room, Martin County Community College).

On October 17, 1963, 57 protestors marched from Green Memorial Church of Christ to the post office next to the courthouse. As the marchers were arrested, they quickly filled up the patrol cars so that the rest of the group had to march to the courthouse to be processed. However, this time, Tommy Bond, a farmer from nearby Windsor whose family was very active in the Bertie Civil Rights Movement, resisted arrest. As Bond was placed under arrest, he jerked away from the

The remains of the colored sign that was painted over the water fountain in the Martin County Courthouse (photograph by the author).

police officer and then attempted to hit him with his fist. The police officer responded by hitting Bond on the head with a night stick. Alma Freeman Purvis witnessed the scene. "We could hear the crack when it hit his head. The blood was just gushing everywhere. That was very frightening. We cried." Bond was taken to Dr. L.C. Wynne, the only black doctor in town, where he received three stitches to close up the wound.

The next day, a group of 35 protestors was stopped at the post office by the police. Only 11 were arrested because the others scattered and ran. Roberta Manning fought back as a police officer attempted to arrest her. The officer struck her on the head, causing a wound that took five stitches to close. "They pushed us so hard, even children," recalled Alma Freeman Purvis. "At the post office they had iron stakes in a fence around the building. I got pushed and fell on an iron stake. I still have trouble with my stomach to this day." After the incidents at the post office, the SCLC headquarters told the members of the movement to avoid protesting on federal property. As a precaution, the SCLC asked for FBI agents to be sent to Williamston, but there is no evidence that they ever came to investigate.

Clarence Biggs, an E.J. Hayes teacher, pointed out that the Williamston Freedom Movement's use of non-violent techniques helped keep law enforcement from being more violent toward the protestors. "If any one had retaliated or resisted arrest, I think the deputies at that time would have used their night sticks, water hoses, and attack dogs. It got close on two or three occasions, but it stopped just on the edge."

Alma Freeman Purvis, injured during the protest at the post office, remembers being scared that someone would get seriously hurt. "There were times when we saw some people getting beat up badly. We can't let people get beat up. There were times when people were ready to take up arms and retaliate. That never really happened, but people did get angry about the unnecessary violence."[15]

One sheriff's deputy was most disliked by the members of the Williamston Freedom Movement. "He would be the initial one to start. He would go into a frenzy; he would do most of the beating," said Bob Purvis, who found himself on the receiving end more than once. One night, Mary Mobley heard her son, Bill Mobley, cry out in the crowd of marchers. When she saw the sheriff's deputy getting ready to hit him again with a nightstick, she offered to take the next lick. The deputy then arrested Bill Mobley and threw him in the back of a station wagon. At the station Mobley said the deputy continued to hit him on the back of the head in a separate room. When Bill Mobley was released, he was so angry he got ready to shoot the deputy. However, Mary Mobley intercepted her son and his friend. She held them by their necks until they promised not to go after him.[16]

Despite the personal feelings of some individual officers, law enforcement in Williamston upheld the law. Sheriff Rawls remembered stopping a white farmer who arrived at a civil rights demonstration at the town hall with the bed of his pickup truck full of peanuts. Denying that he wanted "any trouble," the farmer pleaded with the sheriff to let him pass: "I just come to feed the monkeys."

By not allowing the counter-protestors to become violent, law enforcement was able to reduce the presence of national civil rights organizations and outside media in the county. According to an elected official, "We didn't have any Bull Connors here so we didn't have the violence. It was a situation where we were sitting on a fuse, it had to be primed."[17] Without a "Bull Connor" figure, the commissioner of public safety for Birmingham, Alabama, whose use of violence against protestors is legendary, the media looked for other movements to cover.

CHAPTER FIVE

Jackie Bond

Jacquelyn "Jackie" Bond Shropshire became known as one of the student leaders of the Williamston Freedom Movement through her participation in the protests throughout the summer of 1963. Jackie had a reputation for fearlessness, earned when she and her older brother, Styron Bond, Jr., decided to desegregate the laundromat. While the two were inside, white teenagers took down the "whites only" sign and placed it inside Styron Bond's car. Before the police showed up to arrest Jackie and Styron for defacing public property, the Bonds said, a white man pulled a gun on them.

The police allowed the siblings to take out a warrant against the man who had pointed the gun at them. "We didn't know that black people didn't get warrants on white people," recalled Styron Bond, Jr. Jackie was excited but also very nervous about testifying in court. The prosecutor held up what looked like a gun, which Jackie quickly identified. It turned out that the gun was actually a screwdriver made to look like a gun and the case was dropped. When the judge told her not to go back to the laundromat, she defiantly informed him that she planned to return. Jackie's bravery inspired others. She was so well admired by her peers that the same year she was homecoming queen, drum majorette, and president of the student body at E.J. Hayes High School.[1]

E.J. Hayes High School was one of three black high schools in Martin County. Almost 10 years after the U.S. Supreme Court ruled segregated schools unconstitutional in *Brown v. Board of Education*, little had been done in the county or the rest of the state to desegregate. Through the 1954 Pupil Assignment Act and Pearsall Plan, school assignment was decentralized, which required the black community to enforce desegregation in each school district, slowing desegregation throughout the state. The Biracial Community Relations Committee sent a petition asking the school board to desegregate Martin County public schools. The school board responded that "they would be guided by North Carolina statutes governing assignment and enrollment of students in Martin County."[2] It would take seven more years for Martin County public schools to be fully integrated.

At the end of August, the students returned to E.J. Hayes for fall registration. Ralph Hargett, one of the student leaders, remembered getting to school early that day and placing protest literature on all of the students' desks. When the principal, William A. Holmes, found out, he gathered all the brochures and called for all the teachers and students to meet for an assembly. The principal warned the students against participating in the marches; Jackie Bond Shropshire, Ralph Hargett, and others walked out in protest. The principal tried to get the students off campus by loading the school buses, but the students laid down in front of the buses to keep the students who lived in the country and were bused in from being forced to leave. As 300 students left the school grounds heading in the direction of the train tracks, the teachers were hanging out the windows trying to get the students to come back. "They had been doing a wonderful job for all those years, and it was just one day they could not get us to listen. We were not about to listen, this was ours," commented Bob Purvis. The teachers were alarmed that the students did not have any adults to protect them from the violence that might come.[3] It was too late to turn back as the students gathered to march downtown to town hall.

Policemen were waiting for the students at the train tracks beside the school. The police department's record stated that the police received a tip from TV station WNCT about the protest. Golden Frinks had called requesting news coverage and told the reporter that "he had no control over his people, and they had reached the violent stage." Frinks later told an interviewer that after the anti-parade ordinance was passed, he was looking for a significant event to get the black adults in Williamston involved in the movement.[4]

During the confrontation, an Atlantic Coast Line train started coming down the tracks. The police report claims that law enforcement held the protestors back from rushing the tracks. A group led by the Rev.

During school registration at E.J. Hayes on August 30, 1963, students walk out of the auditorium in protest. When the police blocked the students' path to town hall, violence erupted (courtesy Fred Harrison).

David Carter, the pastor of Bible Ways Baptist Church, tried to go around the blockade and that was when he was struck with the cattle prod. The report claims that Jackie Bond Shropshire fell down and was stepped on by other protestors. Clarence Biggs, a science teacher at E.J. Hayes, recalls treating her for injuries caused by being hit with a cattle prod on her stomach. She later confirmed this.[5] All reports describe the protest turning into a scene of chaos and confusion.

The protestors then retreated to the Bonds' grocery store near the school. According to Styron Bond, Jr., everyone was caught unprepared. White men who were bringing supplies to the store found themselves caught between the police running through it with their guns out and the protestors seeking shelter. Ida Small Speller remembers seeing students coming out of Bond's store with soda bottles and going to find out what was going on. Styron Bond, Sr., had apparently found out about what happened to his daughter and was passing out sodas, saying, "Drink the sodas and throw the bottles."

One of the targets was the sheriff's deputy who many believed used a cattle prod on Jackie Bond Shropshire and the Reverend Carter. "It looked like he was trying to get his gun out of his holster but was so disoriented he couldn't quite get it out," remembered Ida Small Speller. The deputy sustained an injury to his left leg.

Bill Mobley recalled someone saying to him, "Look, they got Charles Howard." When he looked he saw the police putting Howard in the police car. Several people started throwing bricks at the officers. John Small tried to get at a police officer, but five men held him back. The officers were forced to let Howard go as they retreated to take care of their own wounds.

When two fire trucks arrived, the firemen hooked up the hose to the fire hydrant across from the school. Unaware of the water pressure that fire hoses could generate, Styron Bond, Jr., and some of the other E.J. Hayes football players removed their shirts in preparation for the spray. However, only a drizzle came out. Golden Frinks, who arrived in the middle of the demonstration, later told reporters that the hydrant valves had rusted because the town had failed to maintain public services in the black section of town.[6] Several officers and at least two protestors were injured, but the injuries could have been far worse.

A few days later, Styron Bond, Jr., was closing the store for the night when someone fired two shots into its window, following a threatening phone call. The rest of the family was above the store in their apartment. The police later arrested two white teenagers for throwing rocks at the window.[7] The black community understood the warning, that there would be consequences for participating in the Williamston Freedom Movement.

After the incident at the Bonds' store, the Martin County Teachers Association, made up of black teachers, signed a petition protesting the police treatment of students. This was a risky move because black educators feared that they would lose their jobs if they directly supported the movement. School officials rode by the church where the meetings were being held to find out who was participating. Clarence Biggs, who taught science at E.J. Hayes, commented that he would drive people to

Firemen stand ready with hoses to block protesters, made up of mostly E.J. Hayes High School students, from marching to town hall on August 30, 1963 (reprinted from *The Daily Reflector,* August 31, 1963, photograph by Roy Hardee, © East Carolina University).

the meetings, but let them out a few blocks before the church. "I would get as close to the movement as possible without getting fired. We did not have the freedom to support what we felt were our rights." Richard "Gene" Rogers, assistant superintendent of schools, confirmed that if there had been an "extreme case" of a black educator being involved in the movement, he or she would have been fired[8]—just as Sarah Small's husband's contract had not been renewed because of her participation.

Some folks resented the fact that black educators were being paid to teach their children but were not participating in the movement. Francis King felt that "teachers were involved but not in a positive way." Some teachers supported the movement financially or tried to give direction behind the scenes, but they were forced to maintain a public appearance of neutrality.[9] As a result, teachers who were a part of the traditional leadership in the black community were unable to take on leadership roles in the Williamston Freedom Movement.

When school started back in September 1963, most of the students at E.J. Hayes High School and the black elementary schools did not show up. There was also a sympathy strike at the black high school in nearby Robersonville. E.J. Hayes' principal William A. Holmes appeared before the school board on September 4 but could not say when the students would return. The board responded by sending out a letter to the parents about compulsory attendance. It also passed a motion requesting that the State Board of Education give its approval to close E.J. Hayes if the students continued to boycott.[10] If E.J. Hayes closed, black students would have to travel even further distances to go to school in other parts of the county.

One of the main reasons for the boycott was unequal resources. An incident during the previous school year highlighted the inequality between the black and white schools. During the spring semester, E.J. Hayes ran out of toilet paper. When Clarence Biggs heard that the facilities building had gotten a new shipment, he went to pick some up. The manager told him that there was none, but Biggs could see for himself that there was a room full of it. When he asked the manager about the toilet paper, he was told that the toilet paper he saw was not the toilet paper used in the black schools. Bob Purvis, who was a senior at E.J. Hayes, explained in disgust, "We were not even given the same toilet paper."

Francis King, a parent and participant in the movement, said, "Our protests were not about going to school with white children, it

A police officer points at the Baker Gas Company's window which was broken during the student protest at E.J. Hayes on August 30, 1963 (reprinted from *The Daily Reflector,* August 30, 1963, © East Carolina University).

was about getting decent material. Our books were always the hand-me-downs from the white school after they got new books." This sentiment was also shared by Styron Bond, Jr. "We had a good world at E.J. Hayes. The students did not join the protest because they wanted to go to the white high school."[11] E.J. Hayes was a place of pride for the black community. The participants wanted equal resources, and they believed the only way they could guarantee that would happen was through desegregating the schools.

A couple of days later the school board decided to have administrative staff follow the school buses on their routes. Then assistant superintendent Rogers said the reason for this was to find out the black community's communication system. The school board believed that the drivers were spreading the message of the boycott to students as they were waiting to board the bus. According to Rogers, "The bus drivers were not. I am still puzzled as to how the word got out, but we assumed that it was the churches."[12] At the nightly rallies at Green Memorial, movement leaders informed the crowd about the progress of the school boycott and other civil rights matters that spread throughout the black community.

Many of the black teachers did not support the boycott. Black educators like Clarence Biggs felt that Golden Frinks "did a lot of good but at the expense of students' educations." When students refused to go to school, black teachers just sat around in almost empty classrooms. A few students went to class because they wanted to learn, but given the chance, many students chose to stay out. Biggs pointed out, "It was better to organize students in class than to let them run wild on the street."[13] The situation put educators in a tough place.

Substantial increases in attendance were reported on September 10, 1963, by the local newspaper. "Many parents, ignoring threats and appeals by certain groups and anxious to have their children take advantage of educational opportunities, are sending their children back [to school]." In actuality the boycott probably ended because the school board told the parents that their schools would lose money if they did not send their children to school.[14] Since attendance on the tenth day of school determines the allotment of teachers, the school would have lost black teachers if the boycott had continued. Despite the disagreement between teachers and movement leaders, the black school was still an important part of the community.

Toward the end of the 1963–64 school year, plans were being made to start Freedom of Choice, where students would be able to apply to attend another school in the county. Many of the students at E.J. Hayes had mixed feelings about attending the white school. E.J. Hayes lacked supplies, but it provided a nurturing environment. "The teachers assessed your gifts and tried to channel you in the direction that they thought was best for you," remembered Alma Freeman Purvis, one of the first students to graduate from Williamston High School. "They had a vested interest in your future."

Alma Freeman Purvis viewed her teachers as role models. "I grew up wanting to be a teacher. I held them in such high esteem. They were very inspiring just because of who they were and what they did for us." She described an environment in which the school, church, and community all worked together to educate the young people. "That is why when the Civil Rights Movement started the whole community rallied around it. It was like together we stand or together we fall. We had always had that kind of thinking. We can't afford to be divided because we had too many forces coming against us."[15] Students like Alma Freeman Purvis were left with a tough decision to either stay in an environment where they felt safe or be the first to cross the color line.

CHAPTER SIX

The Rev. Paul Chapman

The Rev. Paul Chapman, along with 14 other white Protestant ministers from the Massachusetts chapter of the Southern Christian Leadership Conference, came to participate in the Williamston Freedom Movement in November 1963. Thirteen of the ministers including Chapman were from Massachusetts, one was from Philadelphia, Pennsylvania, and one was from Rutland, Vermont. Chapman, who was serving as the director of Packard Manse Retreat Center near Boston, was chosen to be the group's spokesperson. He told a reporter that the group did not want to "stir up white people. We just wanted to let the members of the Williamston Unit of the SCLC know that we share their convictions."[1]

Chapman had learned about Williamston from the Rev. C.T. Vivian, the SCLC's director of national affiliates, who explained that despite the fact that the Williamston Freedom Movement had been getting "beat up all summer," it had not received any white support or national publicity. Vivian along with James Bevel and Diana Nash Bevel had been assigned by the SCLC leadership two months earlier to research Williamston. The Reverend LaGarge, the SCLC's regional representative, had brought the civil rights campaign to the leadership's attention. The SCLC was looking for a town that offered the combination of police brutality and judicial repression that they found earlier in Birmingham, Alabama, when they were successful in demonstrating the need for the Civil Rights Act of 1964. The SCLC was thinking about focusing on Danville, Virginia, for their efforts toward new voting rights legislation, but they were looking for a back-up plan in case Danville did not work out.[2]

Chapman drove to Williamston in October and stayed three days with Sarah Small. "The purpose of that visit was to make sure they wanted us," said Chapman, "to introduce ourselves, and to verify that we were not outside agitators, but we were being invited in." At one of the meetings at Green Memorial, Frinks introduced Chapman to the crowd by saying he was going to come back with 100 people. "And I winced," recalled Chapman, "because I said, we can get a dozen, maybe." After his visit, Chapman returned home with a letter of invitation from the leaders of the Williamston Freedom Movement.

The Massachusetts SCLC was convinced that outside media coverage would help protect them as well as help the movement. Before the ministers left Boston, they did several interviews with local newspapers and held a final press conference. Chapman wrote in his autobiography, "I said good-bye to my family with no assurance that I would see them ever again, a departure made all the more poignant by seeing television news of that departure when we stopped for supper at a Howard Johnson restaurant on Route 1, driving south from Boston. There I was, kissing my three children good-bye, perhaps for the last time."[3]

The minister arrived around noon on November 12, 1963. After meeting with Golden Frinks at Green Memorial, the ministers were taken to eat lunch with the students at E.J. Hayes. That evening a rally was held at Green Memorial in their honor and then the ministers spent the night at the homes of several members of the movement. Styron Bond, Jr., viewed the Northern ministers' visit as a welcome event. He described the ministers staying in his home and even teaching some of the young people how to play basketball. The presence of the white ministers had an impact on the black community. "It was amazing to black people to see white people marching with us," commented Bond.[4]

Many in the white community were uncomfortable with the white ministers interacting with black women. According to Mayor N.C. Green, "I don't think you can accomplish very much by having white girls and negro boys walking up and down the street arm in arm." It is interesting that Mayor Green used white women as an example, since all the ministers were men, but it does show the concern over protecting white women from mixed race relationships. After the ministers left, a rumor spread around town that "50 to 55 illegitimate pregnancies had been caused among negro girls by white northern integrationists."[5] Again, it speaks to the white community's fear of mixed race relationships as a result of desegregation.

The minsters were taken on a sightseeing trip their first day in Williamston. As the group was walking around town a truck sped toward one of the ministers, John Harman, with the intention of running him over. Harmon, who worked with Chapman at Packard Manse, was saved at the last minute when a woman in the group pulled him to safety. Harmon later told Chapman that despite his military service he "was never so scared in his life as he was in Williamston that time." A similar incident happened a few days later when the Rev. Henry Byrd from Martha's Vineyard was being shown around the town by two black teenagers. "They faced all kinds of really dangerous situations," recalled Byrd. "They were totally sensitive to this kind of thing and knew what to do right away." The teenagers pulled Byrd away from the street just as the pick-up drove down the sidewalk heading straight for them.[6]

That afternoon, town officials passed out handbills explaining the injunction against marching issued by a Superior Court judge until a hearing on November 26. According to the Rev. Bill Campbell, priest at the local Episcopal church, "This was done so it would be common knowledge. We're doing everything we can to give fair warning." Williamston's police chief Lloyd Banks personally handed Frinks a parade application and promised that that the permit would be approved if he filled out the application. The Northern ministers responded that since the parade ordinance was unconstitutional, they would not apply for a permit. The ministers had been informed by their lawyer that they could ignore state but not federal injunctions.[7] By refusing to get a permit, the ministers placed themselves in direct confrontation with town officials.

The first interracial demonstration was held on November 14, 1963, only three days after the ministers arrived. The service was held at midday to make sure that it made the nightly news. Walking out of Green Memorial Church of Christ, two of the ministers, the Rev. Harvey Cox and the Rev. David King, carried three-foot-tall wooden crosses as they led the group along their usual route to town hall. The rest of the ministers followed, each holding the hand of a black woman. Large groups of counter-protestors gathered on the street. A well-dressed white man in the crowd yelled, "I bet there's not a one in the line I can't jerk out of there and stomp hell out of. There's not a one in that line who has been in a church in 40 years." Law enforcement and 11 state troopers stood

W. RAYMOND RAWLS, Sheriff
Phone 792-2589

E. PRESTON JOHNSON, Deputy
Phone 792-3592

Martin County Sheriff's Department

PHONE 792-2868

P. O. BOX 308

WILLIAMSTON, N. C.

November 14, 1963

TO WHOM IT MAY CONCERN:

This is to notify each and every person that on this date, The Honorable Elbert S. Peel, Jr., Resident Superior Court Judge of the Second Judicial District of North Carolina, has issued a temporary Injunction, restraining any and all persons from organizing, leading, or participating in any march, parade, or demonstration in the Town of Williamston without a permit duly issued by the Town of Williamston according to law. Judge Peel has ordered a hearing at 2:30 P. M. on November 26, 1963 at the Court House in Williamston, N. C. to determine if this Injunction should be made permanent.

Any person who shall be found guilty of violating any of the terms of this Injunction shall be in contempt of the Superior Court and will be subject to fine or imprisonment according to law.

A copy of the Complaint, Order, and Summons may be found posted at the Court House door in Williamston and at the Williamston Town Hall.

W. R. Rawls, Sheriff
Martin County

A letter written by Sheriff Rawls to the Massachusetts Unit of the SCLC regarding the injunction against marching without a permit (reprinted from David King Papers, Duke University, courtesy SCLC).

shoulder-to-shoulder protecting the protestors from the crowd. The protestors were led to the courthouse where they walked silently up the stairs into the courtroom for booking. The ministers along with 54 other protestors were arrested for violating the court-issued injunction restricting marches.

In the evening, a meeting was held at Green Memorial. Styron

Bond, Jr., recalls being released from jail in time to hear the speech of the Rev. Wyatt T. Walker, executive director of the Southern Christian Leadership Conference. Walker told the crowd to "go down there and fill the jail. You'll be paying your dues for freedom that way." Following the meeting, a group of protestors marched to the county courthouse where the ministers and other protestors were being held. When an officer asked, "Where are you going?" the

The Rev. Paul Chapman and Sarah Small in November 1963. Small is holding the injunction against marching (courtesy the Rev. Paul Chapman).

youth leader replied, "I'm going home." The group started walking back to the church, when all the girls in the group turned around and marched back to the jail. Another 24 protestors were arrested, making 93 the day's total of arrests.

The prisoners were released individually as members of the black community were able to raise the $500 needed for each person's bail. To relieve the crowded conditions in the jail, 12 of the black prisoners were sent to the Pitt County Jail. A small demonstration made up of people from Williamston took place in downtown Greenville in front of the jail on November 17. Police protected the marchers, but no effort was made by the spectators to interfere with the demonstrations.

In the Williamston jail the ministers were separated from the black protestors, which led to the ministers going on a hunger strike in protest of the segregated cells. The ministers sent a telegram to Gov. Sanford demanding to be placed in integrated cells so that they could "minister

The Rev. Harvey Cox (left) and the Rev. David King carry three-foot-tall wooden crosses as they lead the first interracial demonstration, November 14, 1963 (reprinted from *The Daily Reflector,* November 15, 1963, photograph by Roy Hardee, © East Carolina University).

to our Negro brothers, and be ministered to in turn by them." Sheriff Rawls, afraid of the unwanted publicity, agreed to temporarily desegregate the county jail, which meant that the jail was the first integrated public facility in town.[8]

The Reverend Chapman was one of the last to be released after a week in jail because as the spokesperson he was the focus of the national publicity. Chapman recalled that Sheriff Rawls would let him leave his cell to give press interviews. "He was spelling his own doom, in a way," recalled Chapman, "because all these papers were interviewing us, and we were getting more and more publicity."[9]

Gov. Sanford traveled to Boston a couple of days after the demonstration to speak with the ministers' wives. "Good motives," he told the group of wives, "aren't enough in the incendiary racial atmosphere of a small Southern town, and there are times when martyrdom, however noble, and righteousness stultifies rather than improves human relations."

Police arrest protestors in first interracial demonstration, November 14, 1963 (reprinted from *The Daily Reflector*, November 15, 1963, photograph by Roy Hardee, © East Carolina University).

The ministers' presence among the black protestors helped attract the first outside news coverage of the movement. Jesse Helms, a commentator for Raleigh's WRAL and a future U.S. senator from North Carolina, suggested that the six clergy would do better ministering to their own "racist flocks" in the North. This sentiment was echoed in editorials

The Rev. Roger MacDonald (left) with an unidentified protestor is arraigned after first interracial demonstration (reprinted from *The Daily Reflector,* November 15, 1963, photograph by Roy Hardee, © East Carolina University).

across the state. Ashley Futrell, the editor of the *Washington Daily News,* wrote, "Go home, Yankees."[10]

The Rev. Howard Groover, the minister at the First Christian Church in Williamston, delivered a sermon on "The Crisis of Our Times," in which he called for moderation. He condemned both the ministers' demonstration with crosses and the Klan's burning the cross outside of town. He went on to blame the media for not presenting the whole truth by failing to mention that the white ministers were not local and that they had chosen not to apply for a permit.[11]

The Enterprise broke its silence on the marches to contradict other reports. The editor and publisher, Francis Manning, wrote that claims of white spectators yelling threats at the marchers stretching three blocks near the courthouse were unfounded. He claimed that WNCT had video evidence that proved that the marches were "one of the quietest, most orderly walks yet taken in any racial event. There were no three blocks of people. There was no yelling."[12] Manning attempted to downplay the significance of the movement in the local newspaper to deprive the Williamston Freedom Movement of much needed media attention.

The Civil Rights Move-
ment depended on the media
to spread its message by
showing the nation the brutality of the segregated system. As long as the media was
watching, law enforcement
made sure that they protected
the protestors to avoid violent
images appearing on the
nightly news. After the first
two nights, state troopers
were sent to Williamston to
protect the protestors. However, the media's attention

**The Rev. Paul Chapman (left) and the Rev.
Paul Stagg in the Williamston jail after
a demonstration on November 14, 1963
(reprinted from *The Daily Reflector*, November 15, 1963, photograph by Roy Hardee, ©
East Carolina University).**

and the state troopers could not completely protect the protestors all
the time.

One night the Klan visited Sarah Small's house and attempted to
burn a cross in the front yard. Small's daughter, Ida Small Speller,
remembered her mother turning on all the lights in the house. Harvey
Cox from Harvard Divinity School, who was staying at the house, asked
Small why she was turning on the lights when it made it easier for the
men to see them. Small responded that she turned on the lights so that
the men could see all of them watching. Speller said of her mother, "She
was always skittish, but through the movement she became brave."[13]

Tensions in Williamston were building and reporters for different
news media were stationed around town waiting for what would happen
next. The staff of the SCLC began recommending to Martin Luther King,
Jr., that Williamston should be considered as a site for a major protest
effort.[14] Then everything came to a stop on November 22, 1963, when
John F. Kennedy was assassinated.

The Reverend Chapman heard the news from some black children
as he was walking in town. He and other people in the movement spon-
taneously gathered in Green Memorial as they mourned and prayed for
the dead president. After spending ten days in Williamston, the white
ministers had to go home to comfort their parishioners, and the news

Civil rights protest on December 15, 1963, at the Voice of America transmitter outside of Williamston (reprinted from Daily Reflector Image Collection, J.Y. Joyner Library, East Carolina University, http://digital.lib.ecu.edu/6713).

reporters went off to cover the bigger story. The Williamston Freedom Movement would never again receive national attention.

Sarah Small called for a temporary truce out of respect for Kennedy. A few days before, Golden Frinks was put in jail for writing worthless checks.[15] The movement continued under Sarah Small's leadership.

The Williamston chapter of the SCLC was visited by a group of 100 blacks and 21 whites from the Congress of Racial Equality (CORE) on December 15, the Bill of Rights Day in North Carolina. They came to protest at the Voice of America's transmitter facility outside of Williamston. Floyd McKissick, a Durham attorney and national chairman of CORE, told the crowd, "We were brought over in chains, but we are the voice of America." The transmitter, which was operated by the U.S. Information Agency, broadcast America's message of freedom and opportunity to Communist countries. Since the transmitter was owned by the U.S. government, they could protest without a permit, a fact that Sarah Small pointed out to the crowd: "We want to march in Williamston just as we have been marching here today." The group marched about a mile to the facility; after a rally full of singing, praying, and speakers, the group marched back to their cars without incident.[16]

The movement had started an economic boycott against segregated stores back in the summer. Since not everyone had transportation, people with cars took their neighbors to other towns to shop. The boycott gave blacks a way to participate in the movement anonymously. Clarence Biggs remembered that one of the main goals was to get blacks employed in public places. One of the movement's flyers announced that blacks should not buy anything from "or support any store or business that does not believe in equal job opportunities for Negros." When Biggs approached the manager of Collins Department Store about hiring a black employee, he was unexpectedly offered a job. Biggs already had a full-time job as a science teacher at E.J. Hayes, but the manager offered Biggs a weekend job in the men's department. "He told me that if I worked until Christmas that he would look for another qualified black. After Christmas, he found a black woman name Marie, and she worked there until she retired."[17]

As Christmas approached, the stores were suffering from the lack of business. The Chamber of Commerce president admitted to a reporter that the "white merchants had been hurt severely" by the boycott. The combination of blacks boycotting and out-of-town whites fearful of shopping in Williamston because of the demonstrations proved to be a strong economic motive for the white leadership to end the Civil Rights Movement. Mayor Green agreed to meet with Sarah Small in an effort to work out an agreement to end the boycott. In August, the Williamston Freedom Movement had submitted a list of fourteen demands called the "Points for Progress Towards a Free Williamston." At the time the Biracial Community Relations Committee agreed to meet four of the demands. Four months later the town government had not removed all signs for segregated facilities. The statement of principle issued by the committee reaffirmed its commitment to meeting the demands that they had already agreed to as well as promised to "observe courtesy in all official dealings with black citizens." In exchange the boycott was called off two days before Christmas.[18]

After the ministers returned home, they began organizing a

DON'T BUY IN
DOWN TOWN WILLIAMSTON!
ANYTHING IN ANY STORES DOWNTOWN, UPTOWN, ACROSS TOWN OR AROUND TOWN

DON'T BUY!
ANYTHING IN ANY STORE THAT DOES NOT RESPECT YOU AS AN EQUAL HUMAN BEING

DON'T BUY!
FROM OR SUPPORT ANY STORE OR BUSINESS THAT DOES NOT BELIEVE IN EQUAL JOB OPPORTUNITIES FOR NEGROES

DON'T BUY!
FROM OR SUPPORT ANY STORE OR BUSINESS THAT PRACTICES SEGREGATION -- THAT DISCRIMINATES AGAINST YOU BECAUSE OF THE COLOR OF YOUR SKIN OR RACE -- DON'T BUY SEGREGATION -- WEAR OLD CLOTHES IN DIGNITY.

"GOD IS NO RESPECTOR OF PERSONS"
JESUS CHRIST DIED FOR ALL MANKIND
THANK YOU

The Williamston Unit of the Southern Christian Leadership Conference

A flyer handed out in Williamston in the summer and fall of 1963 to encourage the black community to boycott local businesses that discriminated against black customers (courtesy Styron Bond, Jr.).

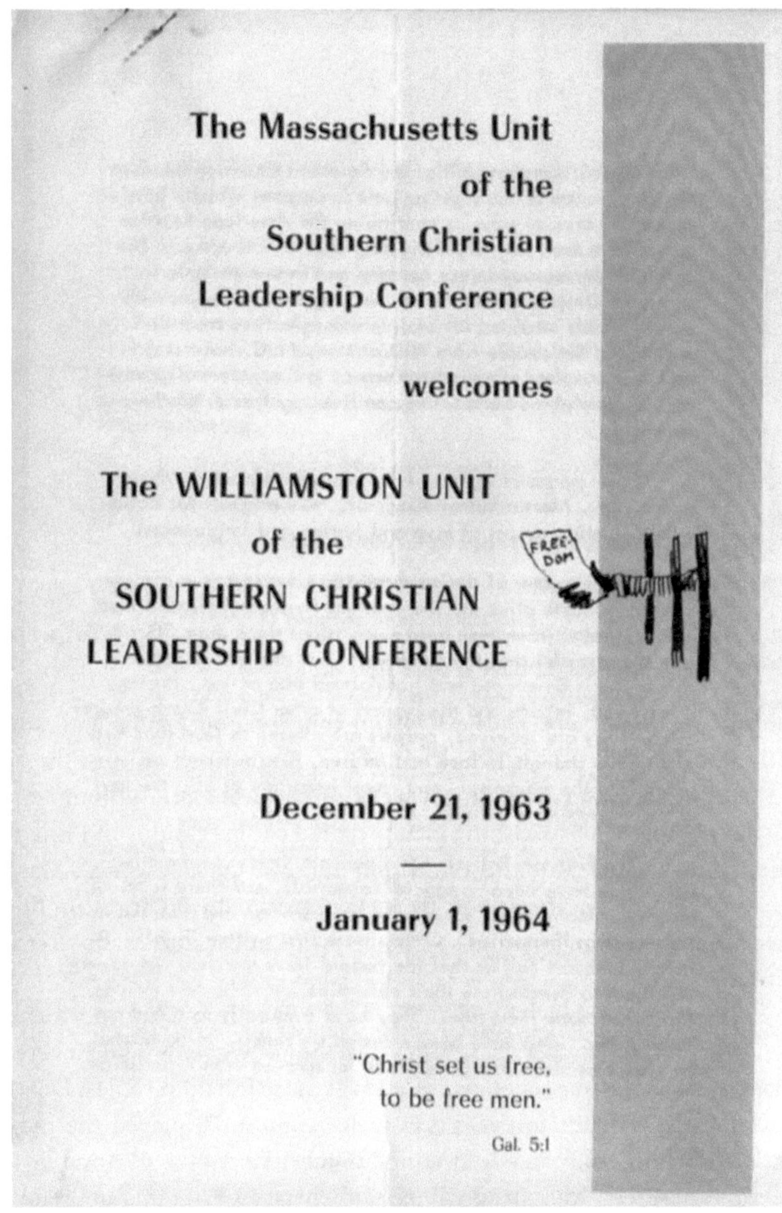

A program distributed by the Williamston Freedom Choir for their fundraising trip in Massachusetts (reprinted from David King Papers, Duke University, courtesy SCLC).

Williamston Freedom Choir performance in Martha's Vineyard (printed, by permission, from Martha's Vineyard Museum).

fundraising drive to bring the Williamston Freedom Choir with some of the local leaders to visit their churches. Once word got out the size of the choir grew to 44 young people. Two buses left Williamston a few days before Christmas; the group visited congregations in Philadelphia, Pennsylvania; Rutland, Vermont; and Martha's Vineyard, Massachusetts. The majority of the time, the group stayed in Stoughton, Massachusetts, about 20 miles south of Boston, at Packard Manse Retreat Center.

Over the course of the 10-day trip, the Freedom Choir performed at various churches to raise money for the movement. The Reverend Chapman was the master of ceremonies at these freedom rallies. Deacon Speller from Williamston said a prayer. Sarah Small played the piano, while the choir sang freedom songs much like they had done at the meetings at Green Memorial Church of Christ in Williamston before a march.[19] One of the student leaders, Ralph Hargett, led attendees in a freedom march through town. Hargett remembers, "Everyone was very welcoming. It was like night and day going to the North."[20]

There was controversy at the freedom rally in Edgartown in Martha's Vineyard when the Freedom Choir performed a song written by the Reverend Chapman that referred to racism in the North. The song lyrics pointed out that there were private clubs on the island where blacks and other groups were not welcomed. After the group left, several letters to the editor appeared in the *Vineyard Gazette* arguing over the appropriateness of comparing the segregation based on custom in the North to segregation enforced by law in the South.[21] Overall, the Freedom Choir seemed to have a wonderful experience on the trip and eagerly shared their experiences with the rest of the community on their return.

Many black families formed special relationships with the ministers who stayed in their homes and white families that they had visited in the North. Alma Freeman Purvis remembered the ministers telling her mother, that if she let Alma go to Massachusetts, they would pay for Alma's schooling. After graduation, Alma went to stay with Father Hugh Finley and his wife so that she could attend Wheelock College. "I was part of the largest black class at my college, there was 15 students," recalled Alma. "I went back into the same situation, it was different, but there was still racism there."

In Boston, Alma married Bob Purvis, who had left Williamston a few months before with John Small. Both men had lost their jobs because of their participation in the movement. The Reverend Chapman arranged for them to get jobs at Harvard University. Over the next few years several members of the Williamston Freedom Movement relocated to the Boston area. Sarah Small eventually joined the rest of her family in Boston and worked for the Reverend Chapman as a chaplain at Packer Manse Retreat Center, where she continued her civil rights activities.[22] As blacks left Williamston in search of a better life, they took with them their talents that they had previously dedicated to the Williamston Freedom Movement.

After the summer of 1964, the Rev. Paul Chapman turned his attention to discrimination in Northern cities. Packer Manse hosted fundraisers for several civil rights groups and became the headquarters for efforts to desegregate the Boston public school system. According to the Reverend Chapman, "My lifetime experience is that boundaries will never be breached by doing the normal thing. You have to break out of the expected routine to find 'the other' on his/her ground."[23] The Williamston Freedom Movement proved to be training ground for people like the Reverend Chapman who spent his life advocating for various causes.

The Rev. Bill Campbell

The Rev. Bill Campbell was one of the few Northerners living in Williamston. He had moved his young family there two years before when he received his first placement at the Church of the Advent, the local Episcopal church. He was from Washington, D.C., which led the Northern ministers to believe that Campbell would support their desegregation efforts. However, when a group of Episcopal ministers met with him, they were very disappointed. According to the Rev. Paul Chapman, who was in the group, "He was not in the least sympathetic to our being in Williamston."[1]

Golden Frinks was released from jail in early February after serving 81 days on a road gang in Halifax. He loudly proclaimed that the local blacks in his absence had been "gulled by token concessions empty of meaningful results." Frinks encouraged the Northern ministers to return to bring media attention back to the Williamston Freedom Movement.[2]

During Easter 1964, thirty ministers and their families returned to Williamston. Answering Sarah Small's call for "Christians—North and South, White and Negro—to join with them on Good Friday in prayer for peace and understanding in Williamston,"[3] Chapman, with his wife Lois and three young children, rented a house on Ormond Drive, in the black section of town, to promote integration.

During the week, someone in town began targeting cars with Massachusetts license plates. The unknown vandal attached a railroad tie to the back of his pickup truck and used it to ram a hole in the radiator of the visitors' cars. Chapman's wife reported that an object thrown from a passing truck smashed her car window. Chapman described the fear he felt seeing a car approach. One day he was walking down the street and a car with white occupants pulled into a nearby driveway. He and another minister quickly approached the nearest house, where Mrs. Peel,

Bill Campbell, Episcopal priest at the Church of Advent (courtesy Manning Room, Martin County Community College).

the wife of the jailer, answered the door. The men thanked her for the meals she cooked for them in jail long enough for the car to drive away. According to Chapman, "Never before had I praised scrambled eggs at such length."[4]

The ministers participated in six sit-ins during their visit in a deliberate attempt to get people arrested. Chapman explained that getting arrested was "part of the game; with arrests comes publicity at the least from the Associated Press." Two Catholic priests, the Rev. Thomas MacLeod and the Rev. John Fitzpatrick, were arrested on charges of trespassing during a sit-in demonstration in protest of the segregated facilities at Shamrock Restaurant. One of the priests commented, "We came face to face with race prejudice which was as irrational as anything could be. Two white restaurateurs admitted to us that it was unreasonable for Whites and Negroes not to eat together, but they defended segregation by saying it was a tradition with them." After the priests were arrested for trespassing, the same priest said, "We stayed in jail in protest—not against laws enacted by a truly representative majority—but against this aforementioned 'tradition,' this ancient and ignorant prejudice we considered a scandal in our midst."[5]

To reach out to the locals, the ministers confronted the town's white community in their churches. Several groups of Northerners and local blacks attended white church services with mixed results. At some churches the visitors were forced to leave, while at others a dialogue developed. After integrating a church service one Sunday morning, Chapman was approached by a group of black kids asking, "Tell me, why did we integrate that boring service?"[6] The kids could not help but compare those services to the much more lively services that they had experienced at Green Memorial and other black churches.

The ministers organized an overnight kneel-in in front of the Church of the Advent in Williamston from Thursday evening through Easter Sunday. The church's sanctuary had been destroyed in February in a fire caused by the boiler exploding. The congregation was meeting in the fellowship hall, next to the burned-out sanctuary. Campbell, the church's minister, claimed that "Paul Chapman told him that the fasts were part of the practice of the church during the Holy Week, but as reported in the press, they had been referred to as hunger strikes."[7] Campbell was so upset by the ministers' protest that he took it upon himself to become the unofficial spokesperson against the Williamston Freedom Movement.

Campbell believed that the Massachusetts ministers had not been given accurate information about the racial situation in Williamston.

Campbell told a reporter, "Some of the ministers have simply been mis-led…. They can strain the situation here by focusing national attention on us, but the people here have got to pick up these pieces. It's easy for them to move into another man's home, wave the American flag and then leave."[8] Campbell felt that the Northern ministers' presence was making it harder for the community to discuss racial issues.

On Easter Sunday, the Rev. Paul Chapman was waiting outside the Episcopal church to pick up other members of the group that had attended service. Four white men drove up beside his van and started insulting Sarah Small. Chapman recognized one of the men as an off-duty police officer, which later resulted in an FBI investigation. The men forced Chapman from the van and slapped him repeatedly across the face. One of the men threatened him, "If you stay here another day, I'll kill you." A young seminary student who tried to come to his rescue was hit in the head with a baseball bat and narrowly escaped more serious injuries when acid was thrown on his coat. Chapman later told a reporter, "In the face of this, we sought to embrace the non-violent response … the Negroes there will tell you that non-violence has a con-verting effect." Chapman claimed that if he had attempted to defend himself, he would have given his attackers the "satisfaction they required." Instead the attackers were confused by Chapman's non-violent response; one of them even sought out Chapman the day after to tell him that he had a change of heart.[9]

A few days after the ministers returned home, Joseph Thigpen, then a county commissioner, and the Reverend Campbell went to Boston to appear on its local news. Haul Reddick, a white businessman from Williamston, recalled, "Thigpen and Campbell went to Boston to show these people we weren't racists." They were invited to appear on a talk show on WBZ, one of the largest radio stations in the Northeast. According to Thigpen, "It was all a set up when they invited us. Everything was loaded against us." During the show, Thigpen pointed out to the radio host that WBZ did not have any black employees. Then the host "cut off the microphone and told us not to talk about the station. So, of course, we did mention it one more time." The next day an advertisement appeared in the newspaper stating that WBZ was looking to hire black employees. Thigpen recalled with a smile, "No one has ever determined who in Williamston bought the ad."[10] The leaders of the white community were not ready to give up the fight.

The white community was not united against desegregation. George Lawson, a recent seminary graduate and member of the Massachusetts SCLC, decided to return to Williamston during the summer of 1964 to learn more about the white perspective. To do this, Lawson lived and interacted with the white community, placing himself in a position where he could listen to what whites thought about race. Lawson later told a reporter that before his last visit he was "convinced there was an evil streak in the Southerners around Williamston, but now I know that isn't true." Lawson had found several people he labeled "white moderates" who were willing to see the system of segregation changed. Lawson blamed the separation between the white and black community on what he called the caste system. He said in order for a white person to live in Williamston they have to "dissociate from the Negro psychologically." By maintaining the system of segregation, white Southerners felt they were doing what was right for both blacks and whites. Without having lived in a segregated society themselves, the white Northern ministers were fundamentally unable to see the white community as anything other than the enemy.

Lawson spent a lot of time meeting with the local ministers, especially the Rev. Bill Campbell. In a letter to the Massachusetts SCLC, Lawson described Campbell and his wife Jane as "sympathetic with my activity." He went on to say that "there is truth in what the Reverend Campbell says, but he was so emotional and inconsistent that I am going to have a hard time believing anything that he says." Lawson wrote that Campbell admitted that the gains made by the community were due to the demonstrations, but that he was careful to add that when the Northerners got involved, the demonstrations did more harm than good. Lawson claimed that this was a reversal of what Campbell had told him after the Easter demonstrations.[11]

At the same time Lawson was attempting to learn from Southern whites, young black participants in the Williamston Freedom Movement spent the summer of 1964 working and living with Northern white families. Some of the students attended summer programs in subjects like biology and English composition. Frinks described it as a cultural exchange. "We took the children to the North to be with white people, to live with them, to see the white people and learn their outlook. We got to get the children ready for social [integration] in the fall. How are they ever going to integrate the schools if the children never talked with white people except maybe in the kitchen?"[12] Most of the young people had not spent a lot of time outside of the South, so living in the North exposed them to white individuals whose views on race were very different from home.

Some members of the Williamston Freedom Movement traveled to St. Augustine, Florida, to participate in the civil rights demonstration taking place that summer. "We didn't realize how good we had it in Williamston until we got to Florida. We got to Florida that morning and marched that night; we were met with dogs, KKK, Billy clubs, cattle prods and a group of angry law enforcement and Floridians," commented Ida Small Speller.

The group was arrested the first day when they attempted to integrate a tourist attraction. Ida Small Speller remembers that when law enforcement found out their ages, they decided to detain them in a local jail until their parents signed them out. "There were 30 people placed in a jail cell meant for only 6 people, which meant most of us had to sleep on the floor; we only had one toilet in the stall and one small sink. To really add insult to injury, they fed us baby food for the whole seven days."[13]

Meanwhile, the adults in the group had been bailed out after spending a day at Jacksonville Penitentiary. Ida's mother, Sarah Small, decided not to sign Ida out because it would be unfair to the other young people from Williamston whose parents were not there. "All I know is when I left Florida, I promised the Lord and anybody that would listen I would never go to jail again, and I didn't. I was cured," said Ida Small Speller.

Toward the end of the summer, Ralph Hargett, the student leader who led the freedom movement marches in the Christmas demonstrations in Massachusetts, was arrested for stealing a friend's car. According to Hargett, after he was arrested the police put a bottle of alcohol on the table and asked him questions about Golden Frinks and other people in the movement. The police were particularly interested in any information about the outsiders who had been helping the movement. When Hargett refused to talk, he was placed on parole until a trial could be held.

Hargett had never been in trouble before his involvement with the Civil Rights Movement. After his arrest, Principal William A. Holmes was left to decide if he could return to E.J. Hayes in the fall while he was on parole. Years later, Holmes told Hargett that there was a lot of pressure on him from the superintendent to get rid of him. Superintendent Manning supposedly told Holmes, "If he separated the head from the snake, the body would die." So at 17 years old, Hargett was sent to live in Raleigh.

Hargett had a sister who lived in New Jersey; he decided to go visit even though he was not supposed to leave the state. When he sent a letter home to his parents, the Williamston authorities had him arrested for violating parole. He was put in a youth center for three weeks until two Williamston police officers came to pick him up. According to Hargett, the New Jersey judge commented that he had never seen police officers travel such a long distance to pick someone up for a misdemeanor. He gave Hargett the option of staying with his sister in New Jersey or returning to North Carolina with the police. Hargett surprised the courtroom by deciding to return to Williamston. "My mother and father still lived in North Carolina. I wanted to return because I felt that I had not done anything wrong," said Hargett.

Once Hargett was released into the custody of the Williamston police, he worried for his safety. When the police officers stopped for dinner at a Howard Johnson's, they would not let Hargett go inside the restaurant to eat. They handcuffed Hargett to a rail above his head and handed him a piece of steak to eat. Hargett stood there in the snow outside of the restaurant and refused to eat, as people came and went from the restaurant.

On Monday morning Hargett's trial began. He entered the courtroom at 10 a.m. and ten minutes later he was sentenced to five years in Central Prison. Whenever Golden Frinks or anyone else from the SCLC tried to visit Hargett in prison, he was moved. The residents of Martha's Vineyard created a defense fund for Hargett and hired an attorney, Phillip Hirschkop, from New York. Hirschkop filed a petition claiming

17 violations of Hargett's rights in his trial. After serving 20 months, Hargett was pardoned.[14]

The Rev. Bill Campbell and his family left Williamston in 1966. Campbell was one of the most outspoken local white ministers. However, his views on racial issues were typical of other white ministers and community leaders at that time. He felt that the presence of "outsiders" was a distraction from the real problems and made it harder for the community to reach a consensus. He believed that change would come from people like himself who worked daily within the community to seek solutions to these problems.

CHAPTER EIGHT

W.H. Scarborough

In 1964 William H. Scarborough was a young reporter at *The Chapel Hill Weekly* who had just returned to the newspaper after spending several months as a press aid helping Democrat Dan Moore win the governor's race. Scarborough felt like he knew a lot about North Carolina so he was shocked when he came across a statement made by Golden Frinks about the inhumane treatment of blacks in Williamston printed in the Martha's Vineyard *Vineyard Gazette*. In a speech made on a NAACP fundraising trip, Frinks claimed, "Williamston is the most segregated town in the United States no different from Mississippi, a place where oppression and economic reprisal, murder, castration, beatings, and mutilation are used in equal parts to maintain the supremacy of whites." In an editorial, Scarborough questioned the validity of Frinks' statement, arguing that if it were true more people would know about the Williamston Freedom Movement.[1]

In response, Scarborough received a letter to the editor from a group of women from Martha's Vineyard. They claimed that they had seen the brutality in Williamston firsthand when they were arrested for attempting to register black voters. The women challenged Scarborough to investigate the Williamston Freedom Movement in conjunction with a reporter from the *Vineyard Gazette*. Scarborough took up the challenge to investigate along with Martha's Vineyard reporter David Lilienthal, who happened to be married to one of the women.[2]

The five women from Martha's Vineyard were Nancy Whiting, a librarian; Virginia Mazar, her best friend and a television writer; Peg Lilienthal, the wife of a local news reporter; and sisters Polly Murphy and Nancy Smith. The women had first heard about Williamston when the rector of the Episcopal parish on Martha's Vineyard, the Rev. Henry Byrd, took part in a demonstration in Williamston with other Northern ministers.

Encouraged by the local priests' example, the women became some of the charter members of the Martha's Vineyard chapter of the NAACP, which happened to be dedicated on the same day that President John F. Kennedy was killed. The local chapter then sponsored the Williamston Freedom Choir trip to the island in December 1963. At the freedom rally at the Edgartown Methodist Church, the crowd was won over by Sarah Small with her quiet voice and plea for "brotherly love."[3]

The women became upset when the Rev. Paul Chapman, having just returned from the Easter protest in Williamston, told the NAACP chapter members about his experience. Chapman explained that many of the poor in Williamston relied on welfare programs because their seasonal agriculture jobs did not provide them enough money for food throughout the winter. So when the county commissioners decided to end the surplus food program at the start of the local Civil Rights Movement, it left many families, especially in the black community, hungry over the winter. While the welfare board denied that the decision was racially motivated, the SCLC leadership saw the county's actions as a way of controlling the black community.[4]

It was then that Peg Lilienthal, the secretary of the NAACP chapter, decided to start the Acorn Fund to raise money as well as to collect donated items for the black community in Williamston. The NAACP chapter held a "can dance" at the high school, where they collected more than 400 pounds of canned goods, several boxes of clothes, and books for the beginning of a freedom library. The women needed a way to deliver the supplies so they loaded up two cars and decided to drive to Williamston. "I was probably more worried about their driving that long distance than I was about anything happening," recalled Virginia Mazer's husband Milton. "They were just taking food."[5]

What the women did not tell their families was that they were thinking about doing more than just delivering food. Nancy Whiting remembered that as she was packing her suitcase she thought, "Well, I'll just take my harmonica along; I might need it. I knew perfectly well that I was thinking about being in jail and that would be a handy thing to have. We knew it was dangerous. We didn't know if we would come back alive. I thought it through very carefully before leaving. But quietly—I didn't talk to anyone about it. I wound up thinking that I wouldn't want

The Vineyard Five consisted of Nancy Whiting, Peg Lilienthal, Virginia Mazer, Polly Murphy, and Nancy Smith (used by permission of Martha's Vineyard Museum, photograph by Shirley W. Mayhew).

my grandchildren to know I'd had a chance to influence people in this way and turned it down."[6]

The choice of five women to participate in the trip was deliberate. The SCLC realized that using Northern white women would challenge Southern white men, who believed their duty was to protect white women. The women, used to dressing casually on the island, put on white gloves and got dressed up. They figured that if they found themselves in trouble Southern men would have a hard time hurting white ladies wearing white gloves.

When the women were asked why they were so committed to helping the black community in Williamston, one of them responded, "Williamston is very isolated, and in a sense the Vineyard, too, is isolated. The expedition is intended to emphasize that both, isolated notwithstanding, are part of the world."

The morning they got on the ferry, Nancy Whiting ran into Bill Honey, vice president of a local bank. Honey was stunned to learn that Whiting, a single mother who worked full-time to support her family, was participating in the trip. The other women were all stay-at-home mothers. "That's one reason I went, because I knew it would have a different influence," commented Whiting. "We weren't just a lot of silly women filling our time." Honey, who was not a supporter of the Civil Rights Movement, offered the women a tow rope and the use of his credit card. The women were astonished by his sudden generosity. They turned down the credit card but took the tow rope, which they luckily never needed.[7]

On the way down the women did not talk much about what they were doing. As they drove, Nancy Whiting recalled reading Thoreau's *Civil Disobedience* to give them all courage. Virginia Mazer, who had grown up in Mississippi and witnessed the Klan burning crosses on the lawn outside her Catholic school, was probably the most scared. Mazer later told a reporter covering their trip, "Once you have experienced the absolute degradation of another human being, you have a new realization within yourself. You have shared the common lot, and you realize that the club can fall upon you."[8]

The women were told by the Reverend Byrd that after they left Virginia they were no longer safe and needed to be sure that they locked their doors. The police were looking for cars with Massachusetts license plates. As they drove into North Carolina, it was beginning to turn dark and the women got scared. "We went through a sort of swampy thing and, strangely, down State Route 13, which seemed unlucky, the way we went," recalled Virginia Mazer.

When the women arrived in Williamston after their two-day journey, they were almost immediately stopped by a police officer who informed them that they were under surveillance. They followed their map to Levester Harris' house, where they stored the goods in a barn behind the house where the family kept supplies for the movement. The Harris family fed them a big chicken dinner and afterward the group ended up at Green Memorial Church of Christ where a spontaneous meeting was held in their honor. Each woman was asked to speak briefly on why she had come. "I remember being the last, somehow thinking

I'd get out of it," recalled Nancy Whiting. "I just said that I felt so happy that they would let us come and let us in because obviously it was going to make trouble. And feeling a kind of warmth and comfort I'd never felt before in my life."

The women spent the night with black families and Golden Frinks sent them out the next morning to help with the voter registration drive. "And this one place we knocked and called, finally someone came shuffling out and, 'Register? Register for what?' she asked in this terribly flat voice. I realize that she'd never heard the words. No idea, absolutely no relationship to the idea of being a part of a community in that way," recalled Nancy Whiting. The women, along with a group of black girls, knocked on door after door, but were unable to register a single voter. It turns out that the blacks who answered the doors were wary of well-dressed white women with Northern accents.

Golden Frinks was unsure how to use his new volunteers. "We had gloves and hats and he just said, 'Oh, beautiful ladies, how can I use you?'" recalled Nancy Smith. When the women broke for lunch, they were asked individually if they would be willing to demonstrate to boost moral. "We had agreed to demonstrate by the time we went back to registering voters, and we knew that we were in for it, because there's no way five white women and a bunch of black people were going to be able to protest without getting arrested," recalled Nancy Whiting. "So I think we were really running scared by then. I certainly was, and that's why that registration part is kind of a blur, because I knew that we were really going to do this."

Frinks had planned for the demonstration to take place at Shamrock, but the restaurant owner was able to close the door before the group entered. So Frinks took the women to the Sears Roebuck store to picket outside against its hiring policy. Frinks ensured the women that, "They won't hurt you." Sarah Small, who had delivered her baby Freeda since she had last seen the women in Martha's Vineyard, held out her baby girl for the women to see. She told the women, "You're going so that Freeda won't have to."

Seven women, the five white women from Martha's Vineyard and two black women, picked up their signs. Sears Roebuck was almost empty at 6 p.m. but a man across the street saw the picketers and called the police. When the police arrived, one of the officers asked the women if they knew that what they were doing was against the law. Polly Murphy replied, "No, I thought I was granted the right under the Constitution."

The police put the women into two cars and took them to the station. The station was only a couple blocks away but the police attempted to scare the women by driving at high speeds around town. "I remember as we got out of the police car to go into the jail, there was then a great crowd of white people," remembered Nancy Whiting. "That was my moment of truth about hatred, looking into the eyes of hatred. It was just terribly shocking. I realized that they would kill us the first chance they got."

While they were being booked, Peg Lilienthal pulled out her NAACP membership card as identification, which did not go over so well with law enforcement. The women reported that a deputy sheriff screamed at them about "barging in on Southern affairs because they'd never had any trouble with you-know-who until we came," recalled Virginia Mazer. "You come from the North you don't know what the South is like, you don't know anything. Then he looked at our driver's licenses and I was born in Jackson, Mississippi. That kind of took him aback."

The deputy sheriff was particularly mean to the two black women who had protested with the Martha's Vineyard women. "Well, here you are again! Haven't you got anything else to do?" Mazer recalled the deputy sheriff saying. "In a sense they made it possible for us to do it. I couldn't have done it without them, their bravery."

The women were placed in two jail cells, the black women split up so that one of them was in each cell. "The cells were just awful," recalled Nancy Whiting, "just perfectly designed to humiliate." The cells had two beds, a lower and an upper, on opposite walls. In the middle there was a little aisle with a toilet at one end. Throughout the night the guards would run their Billy clubs through the bars to scare the women. Outside the women could hear yelling and car horns honking, locals making sure that the women understood that they were not welcomed. Despite the noise, the women were so exhausted they slept pretty well.

That night the women's families were eating dinner together when they got the call that the women had been arrested. The husbands started making calls to anyone they thought could help. Someone contacted

Binnie Straight, who called the jail and told the sheriff that she was the daughter-in-law of Senator Tobey of Vermont. The families wanted to make sure that Williamston law enforcement officers knew that the women had connections to important people.

The next day their husbands wired the bail money to the Williamston Western Union, but the office did not have $1,400 on hand. It took until 3:30 p.m. for Frinks to get the money to bail the women out of jail. When the women were released, one of the black women from the Williamston Freedom Movement said, "Why, you don't look like you'd just come out of jail. You look just like Easter Sunday!" The women ate a quick meal and were escorted out of town. "We left late in the afternoon," recalled Nancy Smith. "It was very spooky, boggy country with just a very narrow bridge we had to go over and we, all of us, thought that once we got over the other side of the bridge it would be okay, but we were sort of nervous leaving there."[9]

Nancy Whiting reflected later, "I think we felt we'd been empowered, we'd been strengthened. That's one of the great pleasures of it because you really lose your sense of self-consciousness. You are a part of something."[10]

Once the women reached Virginia, they felt safe enough to stay in a hotel. "I remember that two of us went into the hotel first and asked whether this hotel was integrated and the woman looked at us in a rather confused manner, and I guess she said yes," recalled Peggy Lilienthal. "We only realized later when we were up in our room about to collapse into bed that probably she didn't even know what integrated meant."

When the women arrived back home, they were welcomed with banners by their family and friends. One of the signs read, "No more TV dinners, Ma's out of jail." Virginia Mazer recalled that the experience was very painful for her son Mark: "He was in junior high, and he said it was bad enough to have a father who was a psychiatrist and then to have a mother that goes to jail."

The women did face some opposition at home. There were several letters to the *Vineyard Gazette* claiming that the women didn't represent the majority of people on the island. "Why don't you mind your own business?" "We'll mind our business. We haven't got anything against black people, but it's their fight; don't get into it. Why do you get into this?"[11]

The Vineyard Five welcomed home after their trip to Williamston by family and friends (used by permission of Martha's Vineyard Museum, photograph by Shirley W. Mayhew).

When a reporter asked two young white women from Williamston about the Martha's Vineyard women's visit, they said they admired their courage but would never dare emulate their actions. "We have to live here. We are part of it."[12] One white woman, Lillian Peele, came out earlier in support of the movement at church and community meetings. Peele managed a grocery store where the main customers were black. George Lawson, the young minster who spent the summer of 1964 learning about the white community, received a lot of help from Peele. Lawson discovered that Peele paid for her support: she was not fully trusted by the black community and at the same time she and her family were harassed by the white community. Lawson wrote, "She is trying to keep her family together and yet still be active in the conspiracy for freedom."[13] While many white residents of Williamston were supportive of desegregation, they remained silent because they did not want to be ostracized.

On July 4, 1964, the five women from Martha's Vineyard were back in Williamston, this time with William Scarborough and David Lilienthal to spend six days investigating race relations. They were greeted by a resolution passed by the Biracial Community Relations Committee: "We hereby demand that all said person of whatever race, creed, or organization decease and desist from such interference whether by personal visits or other contacts."[14] Despite the warning everything seemed fine until the third night. Earlier that summer the U.S. Congress had passed the Civil Rights Act of 1964. A mixed group of about ten people attended a movie at the Watts Theatre to see if local businesses were complying with federal law. Earlier that day the group had been served at five restaurants, including Shamrock, where they had been previously denied service. The theater had closed for three days after the passage of the law, but was open and admitting black customers on a desegregated basis.[15] When the group walked out of the theatre, they noticed that several cars were "roaring" along Main Street. The group was almost back to Green Memorial Church of Christ, where they had left their cars, when the street lights went off. Two cars passed the group, gunning their engines. "We were in absolute pitch dark until suddenly out of nowhere came all of these automobiles with their headlights on, rushing at us," recalled Peggy Lilienthal. "I was with a little girl who couldn't have been more than eight or nine years old, and she pulled me off the road and we tumbled down into a ravine, the two of us together. I really felt this man was trying to kill us."[16] The group was able to get back to their cars with nobody getting injured.

The night before Jackie Bond Shropshire had been leaving a meeting at Green Memorial when she saw the lights on Main Street turn off. She went back to the church to pick up the young people who were walking home. When they got to her father's store, a carload of Klansmen dressed in robes parked across the street. The young people spent the night at the store and Jackie's father, Styron Bond, Sr., sat on the balcony over the store with a rifle. About 3 a.m., the Klansmen approached the house, and Bond fired several shots into the air. The Klansmen drove away. After the incident, Golden Frinks sent a telegraph to Gov. Sanford asking for protection from the Klan. Both the sheriff and police department denied the incident and the governor's office refused to comment.[17]

Scarborough and Lilienthal's investigation resulted in a series of articles printed in their newspapers, providing the most in-depth coverage of the Williamston Freedom Movement. The reporters discovered that media sources were providing incomplete coverage of events in Williamston. The Associated Press had no journalists in the area. According to the bureau chief, "That's one of the poorest points of coverage in the state, and then the police gave poor cooperation." The most extensive coverage throughout the movement was provided by the regional publications, the *Norfolk Virginia-Pilot* and Raleigh's *News and Observer*. Both publications were competing for subscribers in northeastern North Carolina.[18] Studies show that the size of the town, the proximity to a national newspaper, violence involved, and number of police present increased the chances of a local movement receiving coverage in a national newspaper.[19] These could all be reasons why no national newspaper covered the Williamston Freedom Movement.

Francis Manning, the editor of *The Enterprise* (courtesy Manning Room, Martin County Community College).

The editor and publisher of *The Enterprise*, Francis Manning, refused to cover the demonstrations. He claimed that he had a heart condition, which kept him from attending the protests. Despite his health, many news outlets were paying Manning for information. When they started reporting additional information, Manning stopped writing articles because the story did not come out the way he wanted it to, leading Golden Frinks to conclude that Manning had "done more than any single individual to inflame race hatred and misinform the public about the aims of the demonstrations."[20]

Golden Frinks repeatedly criticized *The Enterprise* for lack of coverage and biased reports. Frinks was a one-man public information office, calling newspapers, radio and TV stations and the wire services regularly. The problem that Scarborough found was that many of the white reporters did not trust Frinks. One reporter called him "scatter-brained" and another admitted that they "didn't have a lot of faith in Frinks."[21] The reporters' personal feelings about Frinks influenced the way they covered the movement.

The Enterprise initially tried to downplay what was happening in Williamston. Some of the more violent responses to the movement, like poking Jackie Bond Shropshire with a cattle prod, took place when officials did not think that their actions would become public knowledge. With newspapers like *The Chapel Hill Weekly* and the *Vineyard Gazette* doing in-depth coverage, it became a different story. Outsiders were finding out what was going on, and the white leadership realized that something had to change. "I really believe that if the news media had come in earlier and stayed longer, we would have made headlines in more newspapers and been seen by people across the nation," said Clarence Biggs.[22] It is through newspaper articles that most of the history of the movement is documented.

Chapter Nine

Richard "Gene" Rogers

Richard "Gene" Rogers replaced the former superintendent, J.C. Manning, at the beginning of the 1964–65 school year. Rogers came from a local family and had taken the position of assistant superintendent the year before knowing that Manning had already announced his retirement. Rogers said that Manning did not want to stay through the whole civil rights episode: "He had his 30 years, and it was an opportune time for him to step down."[1]

The plan for desegregation was adopted three days after Rogers took the job. Desegregation was becoming a reality, with the start of freedom of choice.[2] Freedom of choice allowed parents in theory to choose the school their child attended but in reality no white parents and only a few black parents applied to attend different schools.

When school started back in the fall of 1964, twelve black students were accepted to formerly all-white schools. On the first day Marie Robertson, then a seventh grade teacher at a newly-integrated school, recalled an incident where a white boy was late getting to school, and there were no desks left. When he came in, the white boy wanted one of the three black students to get up and give him a seat. When Robertson did not make the black students move, the boy's mother called her, outraged about what happened.

At the end of the day, Robertson remembered, white parents lined up across the street waiting for the junior high school to be out. "We had police and firemen on campus with riot gear on. That was the most

Opposite, top: **E.J. Hayes High School was the school attended by black students in Williamston and surrounding areas (courtesy Manning Room, Martin County Community College).** *Bottom:* **Williamston High School was the school attended by white students in Williamston (courtesy Manning Room, Martin County Community College).**

frightening thing of the whole experience. Nothing ever happened, but the fact that they were there, the intimidation was traumatic for me."[3] This sentiment was likely shared by all who were involved.

Many of the black students were the children of leaders or leaders themselves in the Williamston Freedom Movement. Ida Small Speller, Sarah Small's daughter, remembered, "I didn't have freedom of choice; my mother sent me." Alma Freeman Purvis was recruited by Golden Frinks and Sarah Small because of her commitment to non-violence. "They tried to select students that they thought could handle the mistreatment and still be non-violent," recalled Alma. "When the elders said you had the type of knowledge and spirit that would serve the community, you didn't say no to that. It wasn't that I was so committed. I did it because elders said you are the one."

Not all black students wanted to go to schools where the majority of students were white. Jackie Bond Shropshire, the student leader who had led the protest at E.J. Hayes High School, decided not to go to Williamston High School. When she was asked why she chose to stay, she replied, "My allegiance was with E.J. Hayes. I was student body president my senior year and I did not want to give up everything that I had attained." Styron Bond, Jr., Jackie's brother, commented, "We wanted barriers torn down, but we did not want to go to school with whites."[4]

The students' participation in the movement could not have prepared them for what they faced at school. "The black students were basically ostracized in high school because other students had very little contact with them," Alton Hopewell, a white educator, recalled. "Part of this was their restraint in forcing contact and part of it was the whites' cowardliness to not be the first to make the break." One of these first black students, James Smith, who later changed his name to Jawara K. Lumumba, wrote, "The racial hatred and resistance was intense and unrelenting among a substantial majority of the students. For the majority of the other students, we were treated like unwelcome aliens or disdainful untouchables."[5]

There were a few white students who were willing to reach out to the black students. Alma Freeman Purvis was one of two black seniors; she remembers that on the first day of school, Mary Ann Summerland walked up to her and said she was glad that she was there. Summerland told her, "I hoped that I would live to see this day." The girls then walked to school. Other students threw rocks at Summerland and called her a "nigger lover" and generally gave her a hard time for being nice to the black students. She was angry about her classmates' reactions, but she kept eating lunch with Purvis and Annette Lanier Armstrong, the other black senior.[6]

Most of the white students chose not to interact with the black students. Brenda Whelchel, a white student, said, "Other students would speak to them [black students], but no one went out of their way to be extra friendly to them. I always felt that they were very sad and lonely." Alma Freeman Purvis remembered, "Some students were savages, but most were civil." When it was time to line up to enter the auditorium, some white students would move up in the line so that they would not have to sit next to a black student. "The students who did not go out of their way to be mean, you could tell that they did not have a problem with your presence."[7]

When the black students were assigned to classes, the administration made sure that they were separated. Purvis recalled, "They did not want us to feel empowered. They kept us isolated the whole day." The only time that the black students were together was during lunch; they had to sit together at a table in the cafeteria. "We started moving around and there was all kinds of uproar. They threatened to suspend us. We went back and told Mr. Frinks and Mrs. Sarah. They stepped in and took it from there. We did not have to argue with the principal. When we felt like we were being treated unfairly, they would negotiate. They said your focus is studies, we will take care of everything else, and they did."

Frinks and Small made sure that the students were supported. After school, the students got together and had an opportunity to talk with each other about what they were going through. "They would build us back up before we had to go back to school. They didn't just throw us in there and leave us," commented Bob Purvis.[8] It was this kind of atmosphere that led two black families in January 1965 to ask for their students to be transferred back to E.J. Hayes. The Rev. David Carter, who had been the first person willing to house the movement in his tent church, told the school board that "his son was not welcome at Williamston," but both his and the other black family's request were denied.[9]

In addition to school integration, Frinks viewed voter registration as the most pressing concern of the Williamston Freedom Movement.

Since the "Back Our Brother" campaign, the movement had very little success in increasing the number of registered voters in the county. Frinks received criticism within the SCLC organization for his personal focus on Williamston. Some in the organization felt that he should spend his time setting up more organizations throughout the region. Frinks received funding through the SCLC's voter education program, and it was pointed out that he spent more than half his money in Martin County with only few new registered voters to show for it.

During the summer of 1965, the Williamston Freedom Movement received additional support through the North Carolina Fund, which recruited white and black college students from Fayetteville State, N.C. Agricultural and Technical, and Duke to work on experimental projects in rural communities throughout the state. Lois Harris Greene remembers spending her summer walking the dusty country roads with other local teenagers and white college students to encourage blacks to register and vote. "We were always watching for signs of trouble. To many in the white community our white friends were outside agitators and often the targets for violent acts." At the end of the summer, the Harris family hosted a cookout to reward the young people for all their hard work. A couple of nights later the Klan shot at the house after they heard about the "race-mixing" party. Earl Newsome and his family hosted a young white Duke graduate named Sarah Lynn Wood. "I apparently wasn't too afraid of retribution to let a white girl stay at my house," recalled Newsome. "I remember the KKK shooting at the Harris house. I always wondered why they didn't shoot mine up."[10]

By the next school year, 1965–66, 36 black students were transferred from E.J. Hayes to Williamston High School. In total 105 were transferred to formerly all white schools.[11] However, the federal department of Health, Education, and Welfare (HEW) did not feel that the school board was doing enough. Martin County then adopted the federal plan for desegregating schools, which required that transfers could only be denied for reasons of overcrowding, that transportation had to be provided on an equal basis, and that teachers had to be desegregated.[12] It was at this point that teachers started crossing racial lines.

Since no teachers volunteered, the school administration chose them, putting them through an interview process to make sure that they

<u>Martin County, North Carolina</u>
Public School Facilities
<u>1965-1966 School Year</u>

Schools	Enroll-ment	No. of Classroom Teachers	Pupil/ Teacher Ratio	Grades Taught	Year Erected Plus Additions
1. Bear Grass	344	15	22.9	1-12	1925-51
2. Church Street	532	20	26.6	1-5	1918-19
3. E. J. Hayes*	1,447	55	26.3	1-12	1929-52
4. East End*	848	28	30.3	1-12	1936-54
5. Edna Andrews*	237	8	29.6	1-8	1959
6. Farm Life	105	4	26.2	1-7	1922
7. Hamilton	113	4	28.2	1-7	1925
8. Jamesville	409	23	17.8	1-12	1922-36
9. Jamesville Township*	237	8	29.6	1-8	1953
10. North Everetts*	339	11	30.8	1-8	1957
11. Oak City	370	19	19.5	1-12	1922-36
12. Parmele*	143	4	35.7	1-7	1909
13. Robersonville Elem.	424	16	26.5	1-7	1924
14. Robersonville High	286	16	17.9	7-8	1924-29
15. Rodgers*	448	15	29.9	1-8	1961
16. Salsbury*	218	6	36.3	1-7	1936
17. West Martin*	691	25	27.6	1-12	1951-56
18. Williamston	870	38	22.9	5-12	1952
Total School System	8,061	315	25.6		

* Denotes predominantly nonwhite enrollment.

Source: Superintendent of Public Instruction - Martin County.

1965 school attendance.

would be accepted at their new school.[13] Marie Robertson was among the first white teachers to teach in a black school. She was sent to Rogers Elementary School, along with two other white teachers. She said, "I was frightened at first because I was not accustomed to the makeup of the school. Within a month, I just did not see color." Some people in the black community felt that the central office wanted to send the best black teachers to the white schools, which added to the unease.[14]

A delegation of black parents came before the school board to discuss several incidents between white and black children that had taken place in Williamston High School. Mary Mobley, the leader, requested better supervision by the staff and more police protection off the school grounds. The board responded by saying they would inform the police of the request. Tensions were increasing as steps were being made toward desegregation.

On March 6, 1965, the board of education eliminated all six districts and made the county into one district. Since different sections of the county had different proportions of white and black residences, having one district allowed the school board more discretion on where to assign students. A few months later, the county voted on a $3.8 million bond referendum to build two new high schools to replace the eight smaller high schools spread throughout the county. The bond referendum was defeated, but the county saw a significant increase in federal funds from the Title I program under the Elementary Secondary Act which supplies financial assistance to schools with the largest number of low-income families.[15] At this point the county became reliant on federal funding to operate the schools.

After Martin Luther King, Jr., was assassinated in the spring of 1968, the community came together in an attempt to reconcile their differences. Leaders, almost exclusively white, met in a closed session to plan a march from the courthouse to the ballpark. The participants led by Sarah Small sang freedom songs like "We Shall Overcome," as Mayor N. C. Green, members of the school board, county commissioners, and local ministers looked on. According to local businessman Haul Reddick, some people like the chief of police "really stepped up and defused the situation."[16] Even though some of the white leaders did not support the cause, they chose to work with the black community to avoid violence.

Earl Newsome was one of six black candidates on the Martin County Democratic primary ballot; he filed just a few days before King's assassination. Newsome and Andrew Pierce ran for the board of elections, William Morris and Jephro James ran for county commissioner, Alberta Smith ran for register of deeds, and Sarah Small ran for the House of Representatives in the First District of North Carolina. The black candidates formed a coalition that met often to provide a support group and discuss strategy. "We had the same spirit but we were all defeated," remembered Newsome. "We were running for a cause. There had to be a first."[17] Even though none of the black candidates were elected, their ability to run for office demonstrated the victories being won by the national Civil Rights Movement.

These tensions came to a head when a black student, James Smith, was the top graduate in the 1968 graduating class at Williamston High School. That year new principal Ed Farnell did away with the titles of valedictorian and salutatorian, instead recognizing all the top students. Farnell had done away with the title of valedictorian at his previous school, but now a hidden motive was perceived. The black community became very upset because they felt that the change was made to keep James Smith from being recognized. According to James Smith, if he had been allowed to speak the focus of his address would have been his "appreciation for my family and the hope for racial unity in the future."[18] Instead his graduation became a center of the growing controversy.

At the start of the 1968–69 school year, the black community boycotted Martin County schools. Out of the 150 blacks assigned to Williamston High, only 15 showed up. At E.J. Hayes only a limited number of blacks were present. Instead of as a protest against segregation, this time the boycott was the result of the unfair treatment that the black community felt they were receiving in the desegregation process. Many felt that the black school was losing its identity. Also during this time, a boycott was taking place in nearby Hyde County over the closing of the black schools. The boycott in Martin County was quickly resolved when the board promised to revise the present school assignment plan to allow every student to exercise freedom of choice in school selection. This reversal of policy enabled the students to return to the school they had previously attended and not the school to which they had been reassigned. The board also asked the black community to supply two advisors to the board.[19]

On January 29, 1969, Martin County lost federal funding for failure to comply with the Civil Rights Act. Of the almost $3 million school budget, the federal government supplied $712,000 and the state supplied $2 million. The biggest threat was to the Title I program which employed 92 people in Martin County in 1969. In early February, a three-person team from HEW met with the board and its two advisers from the black community, Earl Newsome and Losa Hassell, to negotiate a plan of integration. The HEW team stated, "Freedom of Choice after September of 1970 is dead." On February 16 the board adopted the amended desegregation plan supported by the state. The earlier plan had been "one-way desegregation." Superintendent Gene Rogers and County Attorney William Peel went to Washington, D.C., shortly after to present the general plan to HEW for final approval. The schools had continued to operate as usual with several federal employees continuing to work despite not receiving paychecks.[20]

HEW approved the desegregation plan in early March, restoring federal funding to the schools. The desegregation plan called for an increase in integration from 7 percent to 25 percent during the 1969 fall term and total integration during the 1970–71 school year. A couple of days later, the school board purchased two sites for the new high schools in compliance with agreements reached with the HEW. Gene Rogers later reflected, "The white community had grown to accept it except for a few diehards. I think there was enough time that it was an easy enough transition."[21]

Elected officials were in a particularly precarious position since they depended on a majority of votes to stay in office. Regardless of their personal beliefs, they had to answer to their constituents, who in the 1960s were still largely white. Gene Rogers, the former school superintendent, recalled several threatening phone calls from the white community that led him to believe that the board was "between a rock and a hard place because of the constituents." Since desegregation was unpopular with the white community, the board members who were involved in the decision to end segregation would have been ostracized for it. The board members responded by dragging out the process until they were forced by the federal government to comply. Rogers said that his board would have appreciated a lawsuit, because it would have taken the pressure off of them. The board realized that desegregation was coming, but they were not willing to start voluntary measures because they realized that they would face opposition.[22] The hope was that, by slowing down the process, the community would have more time to get used to the idea of integration and that outside intervention would take the blame for the ultimate decision.

The white leadership's moderate approach to the movement slowed the federal government's enforcement of desegregation. The white leadership in Williamston, like that in the rest of North Carolina, was careful to use means within the law to maintain power, but was not able to stop desegregation. In the case of the school board in Williamston, the federal government eventually had to step in and force the desegregation of schools because the elected members of the board did not want to shoulder the responsibility. Even though many people in the community felt that segregation was wrong, it took the federal government using its outside position to bring about desegregation.

Chapter Ten

Coach Herman Boone

Before Coach Herman Boone was portrayed by Denzel Washington in the 2000 film *Remember the Titans*, he was already well known in Williamston as the former football coach of the E.J. Hayes Tigers. During the nine years he taught at the all-black high school, his football team won two state championships. During the 1969 season, the team went undefeated despite the fact that many of his players were involved in the Civil Rights Movement. "Coach Boone won 15 straight games because he knew he would be fired otherwise," commented one of his former players, Styron Bond, Jr.

Coach Boone grew up in nearby Rocky Mount and he got his first teaching job in Martin County after graduating from Elizabeth City State: "I came to Martin County as a colored boy, but I was determined to leave here as a proud black man." According to Coach Boone, when Martin Luther King, Jr., was assassinated, he decided that he was not "going to allow 15- and 16-year-old children to fight for my right to be a man." Boone joined the Williamston Freedom Movement despite the risk to his job. He remembers Superintendent Manning threatening to fire him. "I told him, a job in itself will not determine my right to be a human being. He was impressed that I stood for something."

Since Coach Boone was a teacher he could not directly participate in the marches. However, he and other teachers helped behind the scenes with the planning. Styron Bond, Jr., remembers his former coach as someone who "was full of fight and wanted to be somebody."

The players on the football team came from all over the county. Many did not have rides after practice and had to walk home. Coach Boone and the assistant coaches took as many players home as they could in the evenings. "These kids were dedicated. They worked hard

Coach Moore (left) and Coach Herman Boone lead the E.J. Hayes championship football team (courtesy Manning Room, Martin County Community College).

for two hours a day. They were proud of themselves, their community, and they were proud to play for E.J. Hayes."

After the E.J. Hayes football team won the 1969 state championship, Boone was in the bank depositing his paycheck before Christmas break and he ran into Superintendent Gene Rogers. "Rogers said, 'We are very proud of what you have done for Williamston.' Then he tells me that Martin County is going to integrate and 'with you as the football assistant we cannot help but win. I know you have a terrific record, but we are not ready for a black coach.'" Coach Boone was shocked to learn that Williamston High's coach, who was only in his second year teaching, would be named head coach. "I told him I would leave first without a job. I would not assist a man who is ten years my junior. I had a master's degree. Who is to say I couldn't coach white kids," said Boone.

The next summer, Coach Boone went to a football clinic outside of Washington, D.C., where some coaches from Alexandria, Virginia, recruited him. "They paid me $14,788, compared to $3,300 a year in Williamston. That's how I accepted that contract; little did I know that I was stepping out of the pot and into the fire."

In Alexandria, Coach Boone accepted the head football coach position at T.C. Williams. "You could put ten E.J. Hayes into T.C. Williams," recalled Boone. "E.J. Hayes used hand-me-down books from white schools. E.J. Hayes was far more inferior, but its students were the best in the world." The movie *Remember the Titans* documents Boone and his white assistant Bill Yoast's efforts to coach an integrated football team to the state championship. "My hard work in Williamston paid off through the film," commented Coach Boone. "My heart remained in Williamston. I had bought land and I was getting ready to build my house. I canceled all of that because they told me I wasn't good enough to be a head coach because I was black. I took my services and my skills somewhere else." The next year Coach Boone and the Titans were unde-feated, while Williamston's football team did not do as well.[1]

The 1970–71 school year was the first of fully integrated schools. The school board was in the process of building two new high schools, one located in Williamston and the other outside of Robersonville. In the meantime students in the 4th through 8th grades in Williamston were assigned to E.J. Hayes, while the formerly white Williamston High School continued to house the 9th through 12th grades. No physical changes had taken place to improve the schools.

The central office tried to mix the leadership in the school by pair-ing a black assistant principal with a white principal or vice versa. The principal at E.J. Hayes, John Slade, had been transferred from a small elementary school. Alton Hopewell, the assistant principal, described a tense first year: "We had at least 900 students that first day. People were nervous and scared so parents came with their children." He remem-bered calling students' names individually that first day and having them follow their teacher to class.

The violence the community was expecting never happened. "I think what surprised the adults was that after integration, even with the tension, we did not have the violent behavior like mobs or mass break-down," remarked Alton Hopewell.

When the new Williamston High School opened in 1975, a transi-tion team formed to work out a compromise on the school symbols. The black community was able to keep the tiger mascot, and the white community kept the name and colors. One of the points of contention with the compromise was that the black community had worked hard

Dedication of the Williamston Freedom Movement Bont highway marker, June 2012 (photograph by the author).

to buy the students' band uniforms, which had to be replaced by the white school's uniforms.[2]

The black community formed the E.J. Hayes Alumni Association as a way to maintain their identity in the face of integration. "The goal was to preserve the legacy of the teachers and administrators who worked so unselfishly and so powerfully to prepare African American students for the world at large," wrote alumni president Richard Mizelle. Every year the alumni association sponsors events that coincide with Williamston's Homecoming activities. Homecoming is a black church-sponsored event held each September to welcome former residents, mainly from the North, back.

The alumni association also works to renovate and restore E.J. Hayes High School so the community can again use it. The school was built in 1929 with funds donated by Chicago philanthropist Julius Rosenwald, president of Sears, Roebuck, and Co. Rosenwald provided grants to more than 5,000 black schools in the South. E.J. Hayes is a part of this heritage that is quickly disappearing from the nation's landscape.

In 2012, the E. J. Hayes Alumni Association, through a partnership with the Town of Williamston, received a Community Development Block Grant for $500,000 from the State of North Carolina to renovate the school. The alumni association also received the Gertrude S. Caraway Award of Merit in 2013, presented annually by the North Carolina State Historic Preservation Program to organizations that demonstrate competence in restoring buildings that have historic significance. It is expected that the E.J. Hayes building will continue to have a positive impact on Williamston and the county.[3]

PART 2

Oral Histories

The following oral-history interviews were recorded with people directly or indirectly involved in the Williamston Freedom Movement. While it is impossible to interview everyone, the interviews attempt to represent diverse perspectives.

Martha's Vineyard Museum Oral History Collection, under the direction of Linsey Lee, made available the oral interviews of the Rev. Paul Chapman and the Rev. Henry Byrd. The interviews have been edited so that they include only the excerpts related to Williamston. Quotations from interviews conducted by Linsey Lee of Nancy Whiting, Peg Lilienthal, Virginia Mazar, Milton Mazar, Polly Murphy, and Nancy Smith can be found in Chapter Seven.

These oral histories add valuable information about the Williamston Freedom Movement that is not available in written sources. It should be added, however, that dealing with memories can be tricky. People tend to reinterpret their memories over time in order to understand the changing world around them. As a result, people remember events differently; when they do, historians must often turn to written sources to piece together the events in question.

Clarence Biggs

Black Educator
Interview by Amanda Hilliard Smith
October 6, 2005

What happened in Williamston during the desegregation of public schools?

In the early 1960s the public school system was asked to desegregate. I was a teacher at E.J. Hayes at that time. There was a lot of concern from parents and educators about changing schools. Students were faced with violence and jail time. There were not many black people working in public places and segregation was very evident. For example, the water fountain at the courthouse was for whites only and at R&C Restaurant blacks had to get their food through a window.

Styron Bond, Sr., was a grocery store owner. He allowed his property to be used as the place people could meet and prepare for marches. At one point a gun was fired through a window, which sent a message to the black community that the whites opposed what they were doing. Styron Bond's daughter, Jackie Bond Shropshire, was in the front of a march when a deputy hit her in the side with an electric cattle prod. At the time, people didn't know what happened. They only saw her fall. They brought her back to the school and since I was a teacher, I saw the bruise marks on her side.

There were several occasions where the fire trucks were brought in, but I never saw them used on marchers. These were sad times for Martin County and Williamston. I am happy to say that some of the people, black and white, who remember those days are able to communicate more effectively now. The communication between races is better now, but there is a lot of work to be done. There are some who prefer to keep things the way they were back in the 1960s. Both races have this problem.

I am happy to know some blacks have been able to rise above this. Myself, for example, after getting my master's degree, I worked at Martin Community College as interim president three times before being asked to serve as president. As a black man, I would not have been asked before. Also Willie Clifton Peele rose to be superintendent of schools. In the midst of drawbacks, there are a few who have been able to rise above a certain level. Looking back we have come a long way, but we are not at the end of the tunnel. For instance, I would like to see more recreation activities for blacks in Martin County and harmony between the students.

What was it like being an educator at that time?

During the early 1960s, it was hard being an educator. I had to watch as the students were being hurt by desegregation. I wanted to be more a part of the action, but I knew that the officials would find reasons to fire blacks that were too active in the movement. The board members and superintendent would ride by the church where the meeting was being held to find out who was participating. Black teachers were afraid to be identified with the movement. We supported the movement behind the scenes. I went to workshops to learn about the non-violence techniques. I would take people to the meetings, but I would stop before getting to the church. I would get as close to the movement without getting fired. We didn't have the freedom to support what we felt were our rights.

Teachers had to be the first to cross racial lines and teach in the other race's school. It seemed to me that the central office wanted to take the best black teachers to the white school and send us their worst. Some people were asked, but no one wanted to cross those lines. As a science teacher, I wanted my students to rub shoulders with the best. Seeing my students succeed was worth the paycheck to me. I came back to Williamston after graduating from Elizabeth City State. I knew there was a job opening at E.J. Hayes. The principal at that time did not have enough power to recommend me for the job. I had to go speak with Superintendent J.C. Manning in order to apply for the job. I told him, "I grew up in Martin County and I know what the problems are. I want to be a part of the progress of the country." I worked in the schools from 1962 to 1968.

What do you remember about the boycott of local businesses?

At that time we were trying to get some blacks working in public places, so our people would feel more comfortable going there. I got caught in the web so to speak because the manager of Collins Department Store said he would hire me. I told him I couldn't work during the days, but I worked afternoons, weekends, and holidays. I worked in the men's department. He told me that if I worked until Christmas that he would look for another qualified black. After Christmas he found a black named Marie, and she worked there until she retired. My point is that it takes time to open a door. It was a matter of looking at what could appropriately be done to bring these walls down so that we could bring about more harmony.

What role did Golden Frinks have in desegregation in Martin County?

Frinks lived in Edenton. He visited here once a week during the early stages. He knew he had effective leaders on the local level, and he understood that they could provide structure to the organizing. It would have been repetitive if he came more often so he just stopped by. He would often stop by E.J. Hayes and just ask how things were going. He made himself available, but he didn't have to lead the efforts.

He was instrumental in organizing groups. I didn't always agree with him. He did a lot of good, but sometimes at the expense of student education. I didn't disagree with Frinks and applying pressure, but students missed a lot of school. They refused to go to school and teachers just sat around with empty classrooms. Frinks would say, "Don't let students go back to school until we get an acceptable plan or until things are right." He was willing to let the students stay out for a whole year. I feel that it is better to organize students in the classroom than to let them run wild on the street. Frinks had a lot of power with the parents. The parents looked up to him, and they took his word over the educators.

There was a conflict between the parents, teachers, and what Frinks was saying. Some of the local leaders, who didn't have complete understanding for what education was designed to do, felt that keeping students out of school would be the best way to handle it. In my science class, I would have a few students come who wanted to learn. I had one student tell me, "I am not learning anything sitting out of school." But most students given the chance chose to say out. I felt that we should bring the pressure, but not at the expense of the students. I can do more for the students that are in school than those sitting down the street boycotting.

Some of the local leaders would side with Frinks and sometimes with the educators. The sad thing is that some of the parents felt like they were the cause of teachers having a job. They resented teachers that were being paid to teach their children and not participating in the boycotts. Therefore, they would keep their children home to buck us and to rebel against us. I think communication, education, and understanding is important. We saw teaching as the major concern, but we had to yield to parents because it was their children. We had to find a tactful rationale to justify our feelings.

What was the reason for the 1968 boycott?

Many of the parents did not know that the board members were forced to desegregate schools through pressure of federal funding. The move from Hayes to Williamston caused the black school to lose its identity, which led to the boycott. Board members became concerned that if blacks didn't go to school the system would lose money. Desegregation showed just how threatened they were by losing funds. Mr. Harrison, chairman of the board, told me that he didn't think blacks and whites needed to go to school together. No one person can determine desegregation, but they can have an influence. Segregation appeared to them to be a threat to federal funding. The intent was to save the school system and not necessarily to integrate. They had to decide if they could alienate themselves or apply to at least the minimum standards. At first the resistance to change was raw, but everyone has a right to their opinion. How can you hate me if you don't know me?

How effective was news media coverage?

I think that it was very effective. Our local paper made an effort initially to downplay the happenings in Martin County and particularly Williamston at that time. There were people that didn't feel a need for change until outsiders became surprised by their actions. The local media did not cover many of the stories the way that the outside media did.

The news media here did not want to comply and adequately address events as they unfolded. Other people found out what was going on and became surprised. I can't believe they used that cattle stick on that girl. I can't believe they got the fire truck out. I saw some attack dogs in cars, but I never saw them get the dogs out. Some media came in and even filmed the dogs. Some of the opposition to the movement tried to block out the cameras. I think the news media added pressure to the movement. I think that some officials hoped that their actions, like poking Jackie Bond Shropshire with a cattle stick, would not become public knowledge.

The *News and Observer* and *Virginian-Pilot* came down. It was a matter of Williamston making headlines across newspapers other than *The Enterprise* and *The Herald.* The leaders of the county knew they had to do better. Superintendent Gene Rogers, for example, if he thought no one knew what was going on would have felt more comfortable than not doing something or doing something that would not become general knowledge. As newspapers came in from surrounding areas, our local leaders became more concerned about how to comply. How long can you sit out and not comply when you know that the pressure is there? It is a federal requirement, we don't want to lose that funding, and we don't want to be the only system standing outside of the ring.

Could Williamston have been the next Birmingham?

Yes, we were on the edge of what I saw in Birmingham. I went through Birmingham while I was in college. In talking to people down there, I saw some evidence of what went on here, but on a lower scale here. I really believe that if the news media had come in earlier and stayed longer, we would have made headlines in more newspapers and been highly visible to people across the nation. It kind of shocked me to see so many people opposed to doing it.

I went down one day to the courthouse with my daddy to get his driving license or something. I walked over and started to get a drink of water from the fountain that said, "Whites Only." One of the deputies came over and said, "Boy, can't you read?" The point I am making is that we had some real problems here at one time. Golden Frinks went down to the fountain to remove the sign. A deputy hit him right here [right side of head] with a night stick. He put a bandage around his head. You might have read the book *Red Badge of Courage* by Stephen Crane. For a long time Frinks kept that thing on his head, and we called him the "red badge of courage."

Griffin's Quick Lunch was a hard one to crack. You would go to the counter and they would not serve you. What got me ready for this was in undergraduate school I went up to Greensboro. There was a Woolworth's in Elizabeth City and one in Greensboro. We were organizing a team in Elizabeth City. I went up to Greensboro when Dr. Martin Luther King, Jr., and Jesse Jackson were there. I would turn my cup up to get some coffee and several times the waitress would come by and turn it back over.

I can't believe some of the things that happened here in Martin County. Having seen the trucks with the hoses ready to fire on us, seeing the attack dogs in the car, seeing the cattle stick being used, seeing cigarette butts being stuck to marchers' arms. Three ladies in front of the courthouse were seriously burned with cigarette butts, and someone threw rotten eggs into the crowd. Frinks agreed with Dr. King that if you get hurt then just turn the other cheek and don't try to retaliate. If anyone had retaliated or resisted arrest, I think the deputies at the time would have used their nightsticks, the water hose, and the attack dogs. It got close on two or three occasions, but it stopped just on the edge.

What was the effect of the civil rights movement on the county?

I think as time has gone on, the leaders have grown to see a need to work together and become more inclusive. I think our county is better off when you have an across-the-board mix of talents and interests. I think there has been a warming up of the feelings and outlooks of blacks and whites, starting with the demonstration, a great effort to get to know and appreciate each other. I would go to Watts Theater, and I would have to go upstairs. I felt rejected most of the time. I have learned to go beyond that and I don't feel bitter.

Styron Bond, Jr.

Black Activist
Interview by Amanda Hilliard Smith
March 1, 2008

What happened in Williamston during desegregation?

Griffin's Quick Lunch had separate seating. It was different because the blacks went into the front for service. The building was owned by black people. I was at Griffin's Quick Lunch the first time that I was arrested. A customer picked up a chair to throw at us. The owner told the man not to hurt us. He said that it is what we wanted them to do. My sister Jackie rose her age from 15 to 16 to go to jail. I was 16 at the time. The police did not want to arrest us. A police officer we knew told us that we did not have to do this. We were well off, but it was important to us to be a part of the movement.

What was your sister, Jackie Bond's, involvement?

She led us every night. We would march out in twos and pass houses on the way up the hill. I remember an old white woman who sat on the porch combing her silver hair. I would look at her because I knew that we were not going to be coming back. We would be arrested. The first sign of resistance was at the gas station across the street from the church. As you walked, all you could hear was the shuffling of feet. We use to sing on the town hall steps. Jackie would direct the singing. She used to put Mayor Green's name in the songs. One day there were several white hecklers who spit on the back of my neck. I didn't respond because I was there to protect my sister.

One night the marchers were going to Shamrock Restaurant, but I did not march because I wanted to watch Cassius Clay (Muhammad Ali) on TV. He won the fight so fast that I was still able to join the marchers before they had all walked past my dad's store.

What happened when you tried to desegregate the laundromat?

Jackie and I went to the laundromat one day. The ladies in there called their husbands, who showed up. One of the husbands pulled a gun on us. When the police came, two white teenagers pulled down the

"Whites Only" sign and put it in my car. They arrested me for destroying property. I was such a good student that the teachers did not understand why I was arrested.

My sister and I got a warrant out on the white man that pulled a gun on us at the laundromat. The police let us take out a warrant as part of an experiment. We didn't know that black people didn't get warrants on white people. The courtroom was divided into a white and black section. The blacks really thought that we had a case. Jackie just knew that it was going to work. The prosecution held up a gun. Jackie was so excited that she quickly identified it. It turned out that the gun was a fake and the case was dropped.

Were there black residents that didn't want to participate?

Some of the parents had jobs that would not allow them to participate in the movement. Most of our friends would go to Connecticut to work in the summer. Our friend's father sent her away because he wanted to keep his job. When employers picked up black women to work, they would get in the back of the car as late as the 1970s. A single mother with two daughters got scared and had a police officer go pick up her daughters at the rally. She was a "Nervous Nellie." We had on a small scale here "Nervous Nellies" and "Uncle Toms."

What was it like going to school at E.J. Hayes?

We had a good world at E.J. Hayes. The students did not join the protest because they wanted to go to the white high school. At first we did not think we could do anything about segregation. We didn't want to go to the Green Wave [Williamston High School] because we were happy. One day we found out that there was going to be a meeting of the Williamston Unit of the SCLC so we decided to go after football practice.

Did your parents support your activism?

One time my dad Styron Bond bonded people out of jail using his land. But he ran out [of money] before he got to me. The worst part was seeing the family car leaving the parking lot, and I was not in it. He later got a cab driver to bail me out since he owned his own business. People started to bring us stuff in jail. It is not a punishment when it was what you wanted. It was like getting a notch on the belt every time you went to jail. Based on the way I love my children, it is hard to believe they let us participate. Some people say that they turned the heat on us in jail. I am not sure that was the case, but it was hot in there.

What do you remember about the protest that took place during fall registration in 1963?

After school had started back for the fall [late September], the principal was told that we were going to leave school for a protest. We had an assembly where he told us not to leave. Ralph Hargett got up and walked out. Jackie followed and most of the other students walked out. The police were waiting for us at the railroad tracks. Jackie was at the front and one of the police touched her with a cattle prod. Jackie fainted. The crowd retreated to our store. The rooms were packed and the white supply guys were caught in the midst of it. The police were running through with their guns out. The only thing the students had to fight with were the empty soda bottles. They stared throwing bottles at the police and firefighters.

The teachers were hanging out the window at E.J. Hayes trying to get the students back inside. It would have made a great picture. John Small, Sarah Small's son, tried to get at a police officer, but five guys held him back. No one got shot. I give the police and firefighters credit for that. The bottles were breaking everywhere in the streets. One police officer was in a tree and one of my friends hit him on the shoulder with a bottle.

Dad was a World War II vet and he was caught up in all of it. All he could do was put bottles out for students to throw. I don't think anyone got arrested. One black girl got hit. We forgot about Jackie in the chaos. Afterward we had football practice. Coach Herman Boone was in the middle of all of it.

Do you remember water hoses ever being used in Williamston?

The fire hoses were never used, but they did hook them up. When they hooked up the fire hoses, I encouraged everyone to take off their shirts. We were not aware back then of the pressure. The fire department pretended that the hoses didn't work. No one was ever struck by a hose or bitten by a police dog.

I would sit on the porch at night with a rifle. I didn't know how to work a gun. One night some guys in sheets came by our house. We decided to call them nigger first. When they came back by our house, they opened fire. My brother thought he was hit, but they were shooting blanks. We took chances because we didn't know we were in danger. One day I. Beverly Lake, a segregationist, came to speak at the armory. I dared one of my friends to go with me. The white people there looked at us like we were crazy. When we left, we found out that one of my black friends had a gun.

What role did teachers play in the movement?

Teachers were with us, but they did not participate. We looked up to them and put them on a pedestal. T.R. Roberson, who was the French teacher, would go to France every summer. It was something to think of, someone you know going to France and speaking the language. The only people I ever saw were black or white; we never saw foreigners.

What was Coach Boone's secret for success with the football team?

Coach Boone stayed with us seven years before he went to Alexandra, Virginia. He lost his parents at an early age. He was full of fight and wanted to be somebody. My dad could see ahead, and he told me that Boone was going to be somebody. My friends and I wanted to play football, but we were reluctant. A lot of the bigger players graduated and the coach left so we thought we could make it. Coach Boone had us running to the river which was dangerous back then. He never ran with us like in the movie *Remember the Titans.* He always rode in a car. Once we got to the river, we did not get to rest. We had to just turn around and run back.

It is hard to believe that this all happened the same year we had a championship football team. Jackie was homecoming queen, drum majorette, and president of the student body. We would take turns using the football stadium with the white high school. After we started winning, whites would stand at the fence and watch our games. We were too afraid to watch them. Coach Boone won 15 straight games because he knew he would be fired otherwise. The quarterback, Ricky Lanier, went on to play for UNC.

What was the involvement of outsiders in the movement?

White ministers and a few of my cousins that looked white marched with us. A minster stayed two or three months in our house. They brought some students with them that taught us how to play basketball. We didn't know how to pass the ball before that. It was amazing to black people to see white people marching with us. The governor of North Carolina sent state troopers with clubs to protect the marchers.

What was integration of the school like?

When the schools were integrated, they took the smartest black students to the white high school first, but then they would not grade them right. My sister had a chance to go, but she refused. We wanted barriers torn down, but we did not want to go to school with whites. We were tired of supplies that were worn out before they got to us and being bused long distances. Black students had three high schools in the county: East End, West Martin, and E.J. Hayes.

Coach Herman Boone

Black Educator, Football Coach
Interview by Amanda Hilliard Smith
October 14, 2012

How did you end up teaching at E.J. Hayes?

I came back home to Rocky Mount during the summer of 1961. Martin County had a job opening for a basketball, football, and physical education teacher.

Why do you think your football team was so successful?

I think they wanted to win. Winning is paramount in American culture. I don't know any American parents who tell their children to come in second. To take kids who are not used to winning and have them win with dignity and respect. They knew they would be judged on film. They knew they couldn't give a half-hearted effort. They had pride in themselves, their school, and their parents.

These young kids came from all over the county. They had no ride home in the evening. Many of them had to walk five miles after practice. I took as many kids home as I could in the evening. These kids were dedicated. They worked hard for two hours a day. They were proud of themselves, their community, and they were proud to play for E.J. Hayes.

Did you ever participate in the Civil Rights Movement in Williamston?

Most teachers were required by the school board to not get involved in the Civil Rights Movement. When they killed Martin Luther King, Jr., I said to myself, I am not going to allow 15- and 16-year-old children to fight for my right to be a man. I came to Martin County as a colored boy, but I was determined to leave here as a proud black man. I was probably the first teacher to join the Civil Rights Movement. Superintendent Manning threatened to fire me. I told him, a job in itself will not determine my right to be a human being. He was impressed that I stood for something. You can pour water on me and stick the dogs on me, but I am going to fight for my right to be a man.

I was sick and tired of not being able to drink my coffee at the local pharmacy, sick of buying my food out of the window at R&C. I had people of my own race tell me it wasn't safe for teachers to be associated with Golden Frinks, Sarah Small, etc. I told them it was not safe to be a man. Even the principal called me and warned me about my involvement. I kept on because that football team meant a lot to me.

What happened during the school walkout at E.J. Hayes?

I was in the middle of it because I was mad at the sheriff pouring water on those kids. Mayor Green didn't have time because he was playing golf. He never showed up. You did what you had to do. I came to Williamston with the colored boy mentality.

How did you find out about the integration of the schools?

We had just won the state championship. I ran into Superintendent Gene Rogers at the bank. He said we are very proud of what you have done for Williamston. Martin County is going to integrate. He is telling me this in the bank. "We are going to build a new integrated school. So with you as the football assistant, we can't help to win. I know you have a terrific record, but we are not ready for a black coach." The white coach is a 23-year-old, second year coaching. I had been there for nine years, and I am going to assist him because I am black. This was in December 1969. I told him I would leave first without a job. I would not assist a man who is ten years my junior. I had a master's degree. Who is to say I couldn't coach white kids.

I went to a clinic in D.C. and some coaches from Alexandria, Virginia, recruited me. They paid me $14,788, compared to $3,300 in Williamston. That's how I accepted that contract; little did I know that I was stepping out of the pot and into the fire. The rest is history. My heart remained in Williamston. I had bought land, and I was getting ready to build my house. I canceled all of that because they told me I wasn't good enough to be a head coach because I was black. I took my services and my skills somewhere else.

What do you think about the *Remember the Titans* film?

The film shows a man who was willing to stand up for what he believes in. That film is not about football. That film is about how a man can overcome adversity. It just happened to be on the shoulders of football. It is about molding a group of angry and unfocused boys into a football team. Turning them into citizens.

How would you compare T.C. Williams with E.J. Hayes?

My hard work in Williamston paid off through the film. You could put ten E.J. Hayes into T.C. Williams. Williams had indoor water fountains. They had black history; E.J. Hayes had white history. We used hand-me-down books from white schools. E.J. Hayes was far more inferior, but its students were the best in the world. Some of the most intelligent, hard-working students I have ever taught in my life. No comparison.

Where can I find additional information?

Most of my accomplishments were during the time of a segregated society. Most of our history has not been paid attention to. I was one of the few black coaches who filmed their football teams. I have a record. There children can see their fathers play at 16 years old. That part of history, most black history, has been overlooked. It is not unusual that most of the history about me is not around because of the racist mentality.

How many state championships did you win at E.J. Hayes?
Two State Championships and six District Championships.

The Rev. Henry Byrd

*White Minister from Martha's Vineyard
Interview by Linsey Lee,
from the Martha's Vineyard
Museum Oral History Center
November 25, 1993*

How did you get involved in the Civil Rights Movement in Williamston?

It was partly through the group called Packard Manse which is situated in Stoughton and Roxbury, Massachusetts. And Paul Chapman, who lives in Martha's Vineyard in the summers, was the director of Packard Manse, and had a lot to do with it. Paul Chapman had been in touch with Martin Luther King and Williamston was seen as a place that was locked in with no change at all, and people being brutalized. And Dr. King wanted some folks from the churches in the North to come and share with them in the South. Feeling that this would have a mutual impact, that it would help us deal with our own racial problems, as well as help them. It was through the Southern Christian Leadership Conference, Dr. King's group, and they had an active chapter in Williamston and had been trying to make changes there, and were being thrown in jail and attacked with cattle prods and all kinds of difficulties....

I can remember the struggle inside whether to go to Williamston or not. I was doing my visits in the hospital, and I can't remember his name—there was a black fellow in the hospital, and I remember sharing with him that I was struggling with this decision, and he just gave me this big smile and said, "You know what you gotta do," something like that. It was very clear to me that I had to go....

And the local leader in Williamston, her name was Sarah Small and then from Edenton, was a guy named Golden Frinks. He was sort of the area coordinator for the Southern Christian Leadership Conference. And a group of clergy gathered at St. Paul's Cathedral in Boston, and I think it was on Armistice Day, November 11, 1963, and we left from there to go to Williamston. And we traveled overnight and were put up by black families in the towns. And then met at the church there, you know the local black Baptist churches. And trained in non-violence, and were totally under the direction of the local leadership. They told us what they wanted us to do....

I just was tremendously touched by the courage and the spirit of the local community, who faced all kinds of really dangerous situations. I can remember the teenagers who provided a lot of leadership. It was very impressive. And I can remember being taken on a tour of Williamston by two teenagers, and at one point we were walking down a sidewalk, and they suddenly yanked me away from the sidewalk, and away from the street, because a pick-up had swerved and was coming down the sidewalk right at us. They were totally sensitive to this kind of thing and knew what to do right away. Another time we were coming back from the church at night; we were crammed into a car, and the driver started driving all over the place. He finally parked in front of the little black store that had a bright light out in front of it, and he said, "You may wonder why you're not going where I'm supposed to take you." He said, "It's because we were being followed, and I didn't want to give an opportunity for anything to happen." He said, "We'll sit here in front of this store where there are people and the light until they go away." We sat there for about half an hour until the car finally gave up and drove off. But that was the kind of thing people faced constantly.

The non-violent training, getting familiar with the people, and the whole local situation took up a lot of the next few days. And then the non-violent people marched to the front of the courthouse as planned. And I guess the governor called out the state police, or something. Anyway, they had the street lined with police, and when we got there, a big crowd had gathered, and lots of screaming and shouting and so forth. When we got to the courthouse, we were all placed under arrest and brought into the courthouse. And that, I think, had sort of a gallery in the courtroom. When they started booking us, finger printing, all that stuff, it was just—it was very interesting, because it was all done very quietly. The kids started to hum the melody of "We Shall Overcome." Then of course everybody caught on and started doing it, too. Very quietly. It wasn't a loud noise or anything. Finally the sheriff told us to shut up. At least that's what I remember. "No singing allowed," or something. I can't remember how they did it. Then once we were all processed, then we were put in the cells and literally, very roughly, just shoved in the cells. And they segregated us. They put the whites in one place and the blacks in another. And once we were in our cell block, we met briefly and decided that we would go on a hunger strike and wouldn't eat until they integrated us. I think this went on for two days. And it got out in the press and made such a furor that they finally put us together in different cells....

How long were you in jail?

Two weeks. Initially it was really quiet because they threw us in with no gentility at all. I mean, we were bodily heaved into the jail cell. At least I can remember that. And it was very uncomfortable. I think the first night I spent was on the floor, on cement. It was wonderful when they finally integrated us because then we thought we were able to be in better communication with each other, and really learned something about the local people, in ways you couldn't being shut off by ourselves. And I remember we had one fellow who had been in the county jail for quite a while. He apparently was a mule driver because he'd walk up and down the cell block as if he were driving his mule: back and forth, back and forth. And I think our meals were served in a bread tin, you know, the kind of tin you bake bread in. They sort of shoved that in through the bars at us....

What happened when you got back to Martha's Vineyard?

Well, I went back to work. And reunited with my family. But I also ran into a lot of puzzlement, and I think there was also some frustration and anger on the parts of some people. You know, why I was doing this. I remember Bill Roberts at the *Gazette*. He was tremendously supportive. Just a very decent, wonderful guy.... Bill Roberts I think was very concerned and was trying to make sure people understood what was happening....

What do you remember about the Williamston Freedom Choir visit to Martha's Vineyard?

Well, they did a thing at the Methodist church in Edgartown. Had a rally, they call them. And it was to help raise funds for their movement. And it was wonderful. And I think it helped people see firsthand that these were very real people. And they sang their songs with great vigor and told their stories.

The Rev. Paul Chapman

White Minister from Massachusetts,
Spokesperson for Massachusetts Unit of SCLC
Interview by Linsey Lee,
from the Martha's Vineyard Museum
Oral History Center
August 26, 2008

What do you remember about the Civil Rights Movement?

There's a moral clarity about that time that just doesn't frequently repeat itself in human history. We white Northerners were suddenly becoming clear that segregation, that Jim Crow, was wrong, without a doubt. Then arose the possibility of common people doing something to end that. I mean, most time social change is not so available for people who are not directly involved in an issue. In this case it was. There was a call to the North to come south and help....

When I was in seminary, which was Andover-Newton Theological Seminary, I became very close to a man named Virgil Wood, who later became a member of King's team. He was invited by King to work in Atlanta. He didn't accept that invitation, but they were very close. Virgil Wood had been a pastor in Martha's Vineyard....

So in the spring of 1963, I wrote to him and I said, "I know something big is going on." I was living outside of Boston. "And I want to get involved." So he said, "Come on down." So I visited him in Lynchburg, Virginia, for a week, and King was there, and I met King at that time. There were nightly demonstrations in Martinsville, Virginia. And then

Wood said, "You better come to our annual convention." So a colleague and I went to the annual convention of the Southern Christian Leadership Conference in Richmond, Virginia. That was in September 1963. Meanwhile I'd gone to the March on Washington. And so I was really hooked in by now. There were just half a dozen whites among about 100 blacks at that convention.

So shortly thereafter I wrote to King in Atlanta and said, "We have a group of New England clergy who want to get involved. And where should we go?" And I got a call back from his office from the Rev. C.T. Vivian, SCLC's director of national affiliates, saying, "Go to Williamston, North Carolina. The young people there have been demonstrating every night for 30 days with no national attention, and suffering a lot of abuse and getting beaten up and harassed and jailed and so on." So I got in my car and I drove down to Williamston in October 1963. And that's when I met Golden Frinks and Sarah Small, because that had been set up. And I stayed in Sarah Small's house for maybe three or four days. And the purpose of that visit was to make sure they wanted us. To introduce ourselves, and to verify that we were not outside agitators, but we were being invited in. And I got a letter to that effect, that they wrote, saying, "We urge you to come down and join us in our struggle."

Sarah Small signed it. She was the president of the Southern Christian Leadership Conference, Williamston Unit. And a wonderful pianist. And she was the one who played the piano at the nightly mass meetings that Golden Frinks had organized. He lived not very far from there, in Edenton, North Carolina. And he was a full-time paid organizer of the Southern Christian Leadership Conference. So I came back north and began to talk to my friends, and say, "Let's do something." And there was very quick response. Henry Byrd was one of them. It's probably from being here several months every year that I had gotten to know Henry. I think of him as a saintly person. And very, very involved.

While I was in North Carolina, Frinks at one of our nightly mass meetings in introducing me, said, "Paul Chapman's going to come down here with 100 people from the North." And I winced, because I said, "We can get a dozen, maybe." So we went down with 15 people. And that was a very dramatic departure because there was a woman whose name was Phyllis Ryan who was very good on publicity. And she'd worked with us a lot as we were doing stuff in Boston. And she said, "I'm just scared about you going down into that town." And this was a tough time…. She said, "I've got to protect you." So she did this huge publicity thing about our departure, and made a very big deal out of it.

Who were the 15 people who traveled to Williamston?

Well, half of them were Episcopal clergy, including Henry Byrd and Harvey Cox. Cox was a theologian at Harvard who had just come back from a year in East Germany. He was back only a couple of weeks, and I said, "We're going to do this." He said, "I want to come with you, and I'll bring a Southern white man with me," which he did. He was another Baptist minister. Harvey's a Baptist. It drove the local people nuts that a Southerner would be part of this delegation….

We were all white idealists, and we claimed to be all clergy. I don't think we were. I wasn't. But I got labeled right away. There's not a very clear boundary between ordination and non-ordination in that church. So we got non-violent training by Golden Frinks for a couple of days, and then we had our big demonstration, which was pretty simple. A couple of people had made crosses to walk along with, and we had about 80 people in the demonstration, 15 of us white and the rest were all black young people. We marched from the church where we'd been meeting every day, maybe a quarter of a mile to the town hall. There was a state injunction that said we could not demonstrate.

The streets were absolutely lined with highway patrolmen, almost shoulder-to-shoulder the whole quarter-mile on both sides, with such hostile appearance that we weren't quite sure whether they were to protect us or destroy us. But there was enough press, there was national press going along with us, that we were safe. So we were all arrested for demonstrating without a permit, and maybe disturbing the peace, I can't remember, and booked and went into jail.

At that point, the jail was segregated. So all the black kids were put in one cell, and all the white men were put in another cell. A cell was probably designed for about four people, so we were kind of crowded. And one of the men really wanted to protest the jail conditions, but I said, "No, we're not here for ourselves. We're here for them." But we were angry about the segregated jail. So I said to the sheriff, "We're not going to eat, because we don't want this to be a segregated jail." So it made him very, very nervous. He didn't want to do wrong—he thought he was doing right. But if we weren't going to eat, that troubled him. I rather liked him, although objectively he was wrong. So we stopped eating. And we'd never said anything about why, other than that we objected to this segregation. So about three meals later he said, "If I integrate the jail, will you eat?" And we said, "Sure." And so we said in the press, "We've scored a great victory." I learned then, if you're going to have a fast, you don't say, "I'm going to fast until…" because you might lose. You just say, "I'm protesting this; I'm going to fast." And then maybe somebody'll give you a victory.

So we were able to get out almost any time we wanted, because the black adult citizens were quick to contribute money for bail. They were not quick to appear in person because their own situation would be seriously jeopardized, whereas the young people, and the movement was almost entirely high school kids, had nothing to lose. In fact I believe that the movement was primarily a young people's movement. The sit-ins like the first sit-in, in Greensboro, North Carolina, were entirely college students. And it spread like wildfire, almost entirely among college students. And when we had our SCLC conventions and I went to a number of them subsequently, they were all older ministers. But the troops who did all the work—if you see the movies, in the background it's the kids that are getting the water hoses and the dogs, and so it was really a children's movement….

So we got out of jail one by one, depending on who we thought would be valuable outside. And who would be valuable inside…. I spent a week in jail. And it was perfectly acceptable. I mean, your energy is so high. It might not feel very comfortable today, but sleeping on concrete floors was easy. And the spirit was so good. We were surrounded, always, by these young black men who were so solicitous of our well-being. It was pretty crowded. But Sheriff Raymond Rawls would be the primary person we saw. And then there might be one other person on guard. They knew we weren't going to try to escape. I mean, they didn't have to worry about security. And basically he would let me out whenever there was an interview. And I'd just go into his office and say, "It's over." He was spelling his own doom, in a way, because all these papers were interviewing us, and we were getting more and more publicity. But he didn't get it. He wasn't personally hostile.

For the two months you were in Williamston, what did you do?

At that point we didn't do any more demonstrating. We were doing voter registration, interviewing different people within the community. For example, Harvey Cox talked to the superintendent of schools about integrating the school system. And the superintendent said, "It will take 100 years to integrate the school system." And seven years later it was totally integrated. And that's because Johnson had said, "No more money unless these schools integrate…."

Segregation goes only one way. It's pretty remarkable how there was certainly no expression of hostility among the blacks. There was only a welcoming spirit. And one of the school teachers said, "I used to tell my kids all my life, 'White people are all right. You just don't know white people because you live here.' And he said, 'Now they believe it!'" They had this innocent trust about them, yet they had to be constantly on guard because everything was segregated: the drinking fountains, school system, where you could shop, everything. It's hard to imagine now. I mean, a black person couldn't buy a meal in a restaurant anywhere.

When you were in Williamston, how often would you speak to the white community?

We were not welcome or invited to speak to the white community. We spoke to white individuals. There was one quite fun incident. I was walking along a road with a friend, Roger MacDonald, who was a part of that original 15. And suddenly a car of white youth drove into the driveway and stopped on the sidewalk, about two houses away from us. I said to Roger, "Let's walk into this house right here." We walked to the back door of that house, which I happened to know was the house where the woman who cooked for the jail lived. So we knocked on the door, and I said, "You cook for jail, right?" And she said, "Yes." So I said, "I want to tell you, that was the most wonderful food." And for about 15 minutes we praised gruel. And she was so pleased. And the car drove away and we left.

A Klansman came by the house one day and argued with me a long time. He said we were getting it all wrong, that the blacks, they were really very happy. He treated his blacks very well. He was a farmer. And we just were mistaken. So there was that kind of dialogue. But primarily we were part of the segregation. When we would see a car and it was driven by blacks, we'd be totally relaxed. If we saw a car driven by whites, we were on guard. It was that clear….

What were the services at Green Memorial like?

Oh, every night. This was their kind of rallying point. Every night of the week there'd be this mass meeting in the church, which was inspiring and energizing. And people would report all day long at the church what was going on. And a lot of it focused around voter registration, going around into the black community, encouraging people to register to vote. And then occasionally we would be planning delegations to go to white leaders and try to talk with them. But I was much more likely to be in the church. There was a core group that would be there all the time. And then occasionally somebody else would come in.

And then the singing. When I hear "We Shall Overcome" sung I sometimes feel, "No, this isn't the right time to sing it." Because it was always the climax of those meetings. And those meetings had a kind of seriousness and yet joy but this was a sacred song for me. It had become a sacred song. And I didn't think—I sort of revolt when it's sung at inappropriate times. But that song—those meetings were very special. You do share, you do keep those memories. Something like soldiers coming back from the front keep their memories for a lifetime. Quite a lot of it is very vivid, at least there are snapshots, vivid moments. Like when the news of Kennedy's assassination came. I was walking down a rural road and two or three kids came to me and told me. And they said, "We're all going to the church." The church had become such a home for them. "We're all gathering at the church." So we all went there and had a spontaneous service which they led. But it had a deep, deep quality, life-giving quality to it, this whole movement. It was world-shaking. It was part of a national movement that they felt they really shared in. It was strong, strong stuff.

What was Sarah Small like?

Sarah was a very pious woman, but quite realistic. It's kind of a combination of a simple piety and faith. And a realism about what was happening in the world. And always warm and embracing. She had several children—Jimmy, John, Paulette, and Freeda whom she named for Freedom. And those four I know still. And she was an inspiration to all the young people because she was one of the few adults who took them seriously. And she was always at those services, playing the piano. There was a deacon at one of the churches, Deacon Speller, an old country man who prayed every night with great fervor, with very picturesque language. But then I can tell you more historically about Sarah, because she later worked at Packard Manse.

What is Packard Manse?

Packard Manse, which is a residential community, sort of focused on social change. Coming out of a faith motivation, but were too unpredictable for the church.

John Harman, who was there for ten years, left quite suddenly. But then I called up Sarah and said, "We'd like you to come up and take his place." And she said, "Yes," she'd love to come. She came north and became the director of Packard Manse in Roxbury. It was a big house with probably six bedrooms, big old Victorian house. And she immediately won the hearts of a lot of people that had been involved in the program there. I don't know how she got that job at the University of Massachusetts. I mean, she'd never finished high school, and now she was Dean of the Chapel at the University of Massachusetts. And that was by virtue of her spirit. She just had that wonderful insight, kind of Biblical insight, spiritual insight. Was very respected for her earthy integrity, untutored integrity. She always spoke with a great warmth. And she did a lot of stuff. She went to a meeting in Paris with North Vietnamese during the Vietnam War. She toured Israel and Palestine one time.

How did you arrange the choir's visit?

As soon as we got back, we let it be known among the 15 of us that we'd invited the choir up. And I'm sure that there were several people in on that decision. And where should we go as a choir? Because the choir was good. And I wanted to do a recording, but my colleagues said, "We're doing so much already, I don't want to get one more project on our hands." Because we were busy. And so we went around to various churches that had been recommended. We went to Rutland, Vermont, where one of our people was a minister. And we came to Martha's Vineyard because of Henry Byrd. We probably did about six evenings. And they were here between Christmas and New Year's of 1963, staying in people's homes. Packard Manse had enough space to house them all, so we were there for Christmas. And there were two busloads.

What were the services like?

Sarah Small did all that music, and Deacon Speller prayed, and it was exactly what we'd done in the South, each time. A lot of hand clapping, a lot of marching around the church, getting everybody on their feet.

When you came here to the Vineyard, what do you remember about that time?

Well, I was pretty aware of some parts of the Vineyard that were quite segregated. They wrote words appropriate to the local situation. So the East Chop Beach Club came up in the music, as did the Edgartown Yacht Club, and I can't remember the exact words, but a number of the segregated institutions of Martha's Vineyard were sung about in the music. And there was a march down the Main Street of Vineyard Haven. I think, as much as anything, it was the Williamston children staying in local homes that upset people. The Vineyard was more integrated than a lot of communities....

Can you tell me about your visit in the spring?

My family and I rented a house at that time in the black neighborhood. We were as naughty as we could be. I had stationery printed up with my address. And I'd write to all the town officials on this stationery. It was really a challenge to the whole attitude that why can't this be an integrated community? What's wrong with a white person living in a black section?

Around Eastertime we had another big round of demonstrations in Williamston. And by then it had gotten very hostile, and in Williamston we recorded 16 instances of violence toward us. My car was rolled over. One time my wife was driving with my three little children at the time, and somebody smashed the windows in the car. The most common act of violence is that some segregationists had welded a rod onto the back of a pick-up truck, and all they would do would be to pull into the parking place in front of one of our cars—because we had over 100 people by then—and it would pierce the radiator. And then they'd just drive away. It was sort of almost not even noticed. I mean, there'd be a little crash, but you'd look and you wouldn't see anything necessarily, because it might just go right through the grill, pierce the radiator, and drive away. My colleague, John Harmon, who'd served in Africa, Italy, and Europe in the war, said he was never so scared in his life as he was in Williamston that time. The forces against us had really organized.

So as your efforts became more publicized and more like it might change something, that's when the hostility grew?

Exactly. And we never knew what it would lead to in the long range. I think we took a lot of our clues from the enthusiasm of the young people. They were so hopeful. They believed so strongly that this was going to change things that we just wanted to support them in that hope. And not be analysts but just be friends and companions and supporters. Economically, I didn't see a lot of hope for that community. About ten years later I was at a big church service in New York City, and after the service, a man walked up to me and handed me his business card, and it said, "James Small, Attorney-at-Law." But that wouldn't have happened without the movement. It was Sarah's son. He'd gone to law school, and he would have been chopping cotton if it hadn't been for the movement. So the best thing that could have happened was for people to leave, and a lot did. It's just a rural farming town, and so a lot of the young people did leave. All the Small children left.

How long did your relationship with Williamston last?

After that spring when there was all that trouble, I didn't go back. I kept in touch with Sarah through the years. We would talk occasionally. I kept in touch with Golden Frinks. And then what I felt strongly is that we really needed to be acting in Boston. And so we started what was called the Massachusetts Unit of the Southern Christian Leadership Conference. And Virgil became the president because he moved north at that time. And others of us became other officers. And this was just an umbrella that we could do demonstrations. And we did big rallies on

Boston Common. And that group that sponsored King's visit to the North. And then it focused on Boston, on school boycotts. So we did several complete boycotts of the Boston public school system, led by two amazing black guys who'd been to Dartmouth together, Noel Day and Jim Breeden. And they just knew exactly what to do and how to go about it. So we were sort of the support, or the umbrella, for that kind of stuff that was going on. We focused mostly on our own.

George Corey

*White Business Owner and
Member of Town Council
Interview by Amanda Hilliard Smith
July 17, 2011*

What do you remember about the Civil Rights Movement in Williamston?

We had an African American working with us. He was in a Sunday afternoon march. I had a white fellow from up in the county come in and tell me that he would stop trading at my company if I didn't fire the guy. He didn't do any business with us anyway. I called all the guys in; I told them what they do is their own business. If you get into a march and heckling starts, you are going to begin to hate each other. You have been helping each other and there is nothing you wouldn't do for each other. That was the end of it. They didn't participate.

Did you see any of the marches?

No, I didn't.

What do you remember about the ministers from Boston?

I remember the crowd came down here from Boston. An African American lady was in the store one day and she said she came from the neighborhood. She told me that sometimes people would get crossed-jawed over something, but if you needed help someone would come to rescue you. Those people in Boston are not going to do anything for us.

It is easy to say what I am going to do for you if I don't have any intention of doing it in the first place.

What role did the media play in the movement?

I went to Danville, Virginia. They had an ordinance that had been upheld by an appeals court that required people to have a permit to march. It made national news that the police station in Danville, Virginia, was surrounded by sandbags. I went to talk with a police officer about the sandbags. He laughed and asked, "Did you notice the condition of the sandbags?" I said, "they look like they have been there a long time." He said they were put up during the crisis when Kennedy was killed. They never took them down. Lies after lies were told by news media.

A preacher came down here from Harvard [Harvey Cox] to start a demonstration. A guy named Dr. Ruthenburg came several days after Cox came to investigate. He came to talk with me. I spent the whole morning with him. Dr. Ruthenburg was a white minister, a doctor of divinity, who worked for a Northern college. He belonged to the SCLC but his eyes were straight. He came because he wanted to find out himself.

The Associated Press said that throngs were on hand, spitting on the marchers, and throwing rocks at them. It didn't happen. They marched up the hill and didn't have a permit and were arrested. All this news about what happened didn't happen. I called Hurt Campbell at the local TV station in Greenville, and he said it didn't happen. He had video tape that proved it didn't happen.

The preachers had told Dr. Ruthenburg that we rushed to get the ordinance passed. This was all news to me. I called Charles Manning, the town attorney. I asked what date the ordinance was passed. He said some months back. He said that Texaco had a strike in Richmond and they had a guy walking the fence out here. I said, "Would you bring a copy of that ordinance over here?" Charles Manning brought over a copy of the ordinance. I gave the ordinance to Dr. Ruthenburg and told him that I suspected that he had been lied to. Dr. Ruthenburg said that the ministers didn't have an application for a permit. I called the town clerk. He told me that the police chief and sheriff went and gave the priest a copy. I asked him how he knew, and he said that he was with them.

I took Dr. Ruthenburg around town. A black guy had a mule on

Jamesville Road. The news media had made a big deal about him being so poor he had to have a mule. It took money to keep a mule. The guy loved that mule; it was a pet to him.

They had a sharp preacher from Edenton, the Rev. Fred LaGarge. I showed Dr. Ruthenburg the Norfolk paper where he had been shacking up at a hotel with one of the women leaders. He just shook his head. There were many lies told during that time. They were just like politicians. Whatever they said might be changed depending on the group they were addressing.

Dr. Ruthenburg asked me if I thought that any concessions would be made. I said, "Absolutely, but not while the ministers are in town." He called me back and said that they would leave by Wednesday, and they would not be back. The guy who did the lying was a professor of religion at Harvard. The preachers lied to get their point across. I cherished Dr. Ruthenburg. He wrote me a letter, months after he was here, saying he had terminal cancer.

What did you think about the civil rights leaders?

Sarah Small said nothing was being done. I had an *Enterprise* article showing her son in an auto class at what would become the community college.

Golden Frinks was all right. We enjoyed him. He wasn't too educated. I don't recall him coming to town meetings.

What was Mayor N.C. Green like?

He was very calm. He didn't let a meeting get out of hand. He was very steady. We had a meeting one afternoon, and there was a crowd we didn't recognize. Charles Manning [town attorney] told the crowd, "You guys are looking for trouble and you're not going to get it. You might as well go and stir the pot at home."

What kept Williamston from becoming violent?

Leadership. When we had a meeting there wasn't any demonstration. I can see where you would have a rabble-rouser mayor or town board. It just didn't happen.

Was there a Klan presence here?

I knew of one man who was an advocate before the demonstrations started. He didn't talk about it much to me. I don't think they had a vivid presence here. I don't remember any meetings. I am satisfied that some conversations took place that I didn't hear. I was on the town board and I believed in being fair.

Lois Harris Greene

Black Activist
Interview by Amanda Hilliard Smith
November 10, 2012

How did you get involved in the movement?

I was always at the mass meetings because my mother was involved. I don't believe we missed a meeting at Green Memorial. My mother, Levester Downey Harris, acted as secretary of the Williamston SCLC movement. She never was arrested in Martin County. Part of her responsibility was to arrange bonds for those who were jailed. Ironically, she traveled to Florida along with Mr. Frinks and others and was arrested there.

A white minister and I were arrested for sitting after being refused service at Shamrock Restaurant. As soon as we were taken off two others went in. Before it was over four teenage girls—Blondell Mobley, Mary Clemmons, Alma Freeman, and myself—were locked in a cell with four beds and just enough walking space to get to the toilet. We could have been bailed out at any time, but we chose to stay. I stayed seven days. Most of the time we were hungry. Alma Freeman began to sing a song in the tune of "Just a Closer Walk with Thee." It went, "Just a bowl of black-eyed peas, and a piece of cornbread, please, and a piece of fatback too; Let it be, dear Lord, let it be. Just a mattress for my bed, and a pillow for my head, and a blanket over me; Let it be, dear Lord, let it be."

What did you remember about the 1963 boycott?

My dad ran a grocery store. All my relatives went to Washington to buy groceries. The ministers brought non-perishable food and clothing. My parents set up a utility barn in our backyard, which became the distribution center.

Did you participate in the Freedom Choir?

I, along with others, sang in our Freedom Choir under the musical direction of Mrs. Sarah. The Freedom Choir toured parts of Massachusetts, Vermont, and Maine. The highlight of the trip for me was Martha's Vineyard.

What was your experience like at Williamston High School?

I spent the summer of 1964 in Massachusetts. When I returned home one of the first things my mom told me was that I was going to Williamston High School. It really was not what I wanted to do but the cause was greater than my desires. Thus, I began my junior year at Williamston High School. I can remember the first day that I went into my homeroom. I sat in the middle of the room and everyone else scattered to the outside of the room. The teacher seated them in alphabetical order. Over time it got better but there were always kids that picked and called us names. I would fight. I had a mouth. They thought I was crazy and they wouldn't bother me. They would pick on James "Jody" Smith. I had a car and I would drive behind him so they could not beat up Jody. He was small and timid.

What did you do during the summer of 1965?

During the summer of 1965, I along with other area teenagers and white college students logged many hours walking dusty country roads knocking on doors encouraging blacks to register and vote. We were always watching for signs of trouble. Too many in the white community viewed our white friends as "outside agitators" and often the target of violent acts. Toward the end of the summer my mom and other movement leaders decided we had worked hard and deserved a little reward. My mother pulled out the grill. We set up the music under the carport and became carefree teenagers for an hour or two.

A couple of nights following that cook out the Klan drove by our house and shot through my parents' bedroom window. It was our belief that one of the delivery men told the Klan of the race-mixing party. My father drove around with a bullet hole in his car until he traded it in.

Ralph Hargett

Black Activist
Interview by Amanda Hilliard Smith
October 29, 2012

What do you remember about the Williamston Freedom Movement?

I was appointed a youth leader for the school. I would be the first one at school in the morning to place the literature on each child's desk at the high school. One morning the principal came in and gathered up my brochures. He called everyone to meet in the gym. He and some other teachers gave a speech. He said that anyone who left the school campus today would be expelled for the rest of the year. This was September. I stood up and said we had planned to go downtown today and demonstrate. We knew it was noon because we heard the sawmill whistle. I walked out and the rest of the school from 7th grade and up walked out.

The principal didn't want us to go; he did everything in his power to stop us from going. We even lay down in front of the school buses to keep the buses from taking the people who lived in the countryside home. The police launched a brutal assault with bull clubs and pushed us back to the campus. Then bottles and glass started to fly. The police would try to block the bottles from coming, and they were getting cut. It was all documented on WITN news.

Shortly after walking out of school, two FBI agents came and got me out of school. They threatened to throw me into the Roanoke River. They had me go with them without contacting my parents or anyone.

What do you remember about the trip to Massachusetts?

We all stayed at a lodge in Massachusetts. We would go to different churches and rallies. I remember ringing a bell in Martha's Vineyard to call the service to order and pulling the bell out of the steeple. Luckily no one was hurt. We met some real nice people; they separated us in groups and we would stay with families. We would come together for meetings at night. We drew some really nice crowds. The Martha's Vineyard people were very welcoming. You could feel the love. It was like night and day going to the North and being treated that way. It was nothing like the snobbish treatment we were getting in the South.

What happened when you were arrested for stealing a car in 1964?

I moved back to Williamston in 1979. I guess it was six months before our principal died. He explained to me what happened when I got arrested for stealing a friend's car. I had never been in trouble before. The decision was placed on the principal whether I could come back to school or be sent to jail. He told me that there was pressure on him to get rid of me. The superintendent told him that if you separate the head from the snake, the body would die. His recommendation was that I would go to prison.

The first time they released me on parole, they gave me a job in Raleigh. I was 17 years old at the time and living at the YMCA. I left the state to go to New Jersey to live with my sister. They found me because I sent a letter to my mother. They arrested me in New Jersey and put me in a youth center. I was there 2 or 3 weeks before Williamston police came to get me. The judge gave me the option to stay with my sister in New Jersey or return to North Carolina with the police. My mother and father were still in North Carolina. My mother was working at the white high school, and she was getting threats. I wanted to return to North Carolina because I felt that I hadn't done anything. The judge said that I did not have to return. He had never seen anything like it. He couldn't believe police officers come all the way to New Jersey for a misdemeanor.

It was snowing on the way back. On the New Jersey Turnpike, we stopped at a Howard Johnson's. The police handcuffed me to a rail above my head and in the other hand they gave me a steak. They pulled their coats off so people could see their guns. They wouldn't let me go inside the restaurant. Then we continued to go south. They would take the revolvers out and put the gun to my head. During interrogation they put a bottle in front of me. They were trying to get information on other people, especially about the outsiders coming in to help us with the struggle.

They got me back over the weekend, I went to the court room on Monday at 10 a.m., and ten minutes later I walked out with five years. At the time period, the maximum sentence for my offense was 30 days.

They sent me to central prison. Every time the SCLC tried to come to interview me, they would find out that they were coming and they would send me to another camp. I did about 20 months before I was given a pardon. James Latham, the other person who was arrested, was released a year before me. He was given a pardon and moved to back Philadelphia.

After I finished high school, I went into the Marine Corps and went to Vietnam. I did end up writing a congressman and there was a big investigation into my arrest. I am a lifelong activist.

Alton Hopewell

White Teacher
Interview by Amanda Hilliard Smith
June 22, 2005

What do you remember of desegregation in Williamston?

Nineteen sixty-three was the summer of the protest. From an outsider's point of view, it was like a carnival scene with the marches taking place every night. We could hear the noise of people clapping and the marching band from our house. One of the student drum majors, who was famous for his height, would lead the march. The crowd would sing spirituals like "We Shall Overcome."

The Episcopal church from Massachusetts came down as part of the protest. The group was made up of both white women and men. NBC news covered the event and pictured the town as backwards. For instance, they did a feature on an elderly black man that still drove around in a mule and cart.

That summer the North Carolina legislature adopted the Pearsall plan. Mr. Pearsall was from Rocky Mount, and he proposed a policy that called for freedom of choice. Under this policy, the students were allowed to choose the school they wanted to attend in their district. If there weren't multiple schools in their district, then they had no real choice. In Martin County there was a black and white school in each district. I started teaching in Williamston in the 1963–64 school year.

When we came back in the fall, there were about a dozen students from Hayes that filed to attend Williamston High School. No white students chose to go to Hayes. I guess that is what people would have expected. That year they began intermingling of teachers at the school. I don't guess it was compulsory. They received three or four volunteers from white teachers to go to work at Hayes. They had at least three very good black teachers from Hayes come to Williamston. There was Ms. Gillman, an English teacher; Mr. Roberson, a French teacher; and someone else. They did very well at Williamston and the students did very well with them.

That pattern was followed until 1970, when the county, under court order and legislative pressure, was told to play the game right under a unified school system. Up until that, everyone understood that in the South you had a dual school system. It was basically the 1954 *Brown v. Board* decision and the 1964 Civil Rights Act that were part of the pressure. The Office of Civil Rights also ordered all Southern states to create a unified school system. They said that the law had been set in 1954, and you hadn't done much about it.

Let's talk about the 12 black students that went to the white school. Some of the students did well; I mean personally. I am not talking just about their grades. They were basically ostracized in high school because other students had very little contact with them. I had several in my class, and I saw how they sat by themselves. Part of this was their restraint in forcing contact and part of it was the whites' cowardliness to not be the first to make the break.

I was teaching physics that year, and I had one black girl in my class named Annette Armstrong Lanier. A white student named Marianne Summerlynn, who was a good student and cared about people, did eat lunch with two of the black girls. She got some very terrible notes from other students, and they gave her a hard time for making any social overtures. She was very angry about it, but she continued to be friendly to the girls. I remember one day while the Lanier girl was absent from my class, I took the opportunity to talk to the class about the treatment and vent a little bit about the situation. Summerlynn was very angry because she didn't want the class talking about Annett Armstrong Lanier while she wasn't there.

After the second and third year this went on, I know that a couple of the black students felt the pressure was too much, and they went back to E.J. Hayes. One of them later became a teacher at Williamston High School, so I talked with her about it years later. She was a good student, and I tried not to treat her any differently in my algebra class. She said she respected that, but the whole atmosphere she just didn't like.

In 1967–68 the top student in the senior class was a black student named James Smith, who is a lawyer now. He came to school every day with a briefcase, and he got a lot of flak for that. During the time the principal resigned and was replaced by Mr. Farnell. Mr. Farnell felt that you should not have valedictorians and salutatorians because all the grades are so close. He created the honor student system that we still have today. This happened to come about the year that James would have been the salutatorian. There was a lot of flak about that from the black community because they felt Mr. Farnell did that to keep James from being recognized. I don't think he did. I agreed with his reasoning that all the top graduates should be recognized.

Nineteen seventy was the year we fully integrated the schools. I went to Hayes as the assistant principal which was then the 4th through 8th grade school. They took each district and without adding any new buildings they reassigned all the students. So they had to use the building in odd ways to accommodate all the students.

What was full integration like?

They made this decision in the summer, and they did things that were not satisfactory for anybody. The majority of the whites didn't want to integrate, and the majority of the blacks probably were afraid of it even though the political leadership was fighting for it. They made the four white high schools into the integrated high schools in every case and left the white principals. They turned the black high schools into middle or elementary schools depending on the population in that district. In most cases, they left the black principals at those schools. They tried to create mixed leadership by putting black assistant principals with white principals. That is the reason I became the assistant principal at Hayes even though I had no interest in being a principal. I agreed to go because I thought it would help out some.

We started at Hayes with only a few days to get the buildings ready.

The principal, Mr. Slade, had been transferred in from a small elementary school to a very large school. We had at least 900 students that first day. There had been no open house or introduction to the building prior to the first day of school. It was a very hot day in September. We had all the student body and parents meet in the gym. People were nervous and scared so parents came with their children. We organized the school by calling out the names of every student and had them follow their teacher to the classroom. It was a long ordeal, but we got through it with no real trouble.

The back building was new but the front building was very old. There was not a water fountain in the whole school; there was a cement bench in the front with spigots. But that was it. There were too many students to feed in the cafeteria and we were just overcrowded with the space we had. People in the community did the extras for the schools like building gyms. Since there was such a difference in the economics of the black community, their schools lacked things like water fountains.

Sometimes throughout the year, there was a day or two when black students would say that they were not going to class. The principal usually managed to get the students that wouldn't go to class to go home. Sometimes there would be racial problems at the high school, and parents would come to Hayes to pick up our students. I don't recall that it was ever more than one or two, and it didn't cause a problem. I think what surprised the adults was that after integration even with the tension, we did not have the violent behavior like mobs or mass break down. I think a lot of people thought that was going to happen. There was a lot of mistrust and fear that a teacher would be prejudiced against a student of different race.

Mr. Slate was an easy-going man, and everyone worked with him through a tough situation. At the beginning of the year there were a lot of things that were not ready like the books. Today you do a lot more preparation, but there just wasn't time.

What was desegregation like in other parts of the county?

In Jamesville and Bear Grass, there wasn't a black high school so these students were assigned to a school district that they had never attended. Since that was a small school, they didn't have the crowding problems like Williamston. In those days the smart black students went to Hayes, but over half didn't continue school past the eight grade. A lot of the students had to work on the farms and that controlled the size of the high schools.

Oak City had a black and white high school. The black school had the better building, but it still became the elementary. The high school closed in 1975 when Roanoke High School was built and the elementary school is still open. Only one year earlier the new Williamston High School was built. In Robersonville the white high school became the middle school and the black high school is the elementary school. The high school students go to the new Roanoke High. In 1970 a private academy started in Everetts called Martin Academy. That lasted about ten years until it folded. Students came there from all over the county, but mostly Robersonville and Hamilton. Four schools were built in the 1920s: Jamesville, Williamston Primary, Farm Life, and Oak City. They replaced one-room schoolhouses. Before then, the only high school was in Williamston, and students had to move to Williamston to continue their education.

Hayes teachers put a lot of effort into students; they singled out students with special talents. It is amazing how many doctors and lawyers came from that school. These students came from families that didn't have the educational background to get ahead, and it was the teachers that got them to college.

Frances King

Black Leader
Interview by Amanda Hilliard Smith
October 22, 2005

What happened in Williamston during desegregation?

I remember the first Sunday we marched was June 30, 1963. My husband and I were singing in his choir in Ahoskie, and we had to leave early to get back to Williamston in time for the march. The participants in the march were mostly youth. I was 26 at the time and one of the oldest marchers. We would march downtown, and it was peaceful.

I remember it well because my cousin, Sarah Small, was president of the SCLC and a musician. She was a mentor to me. When my mom died early, she became like a mother to me. Small was very religious and later went on to become the Baptist chaplin at the University of Massachusetts. That is where she lived after she left Williamston.

We were protesting in Williamston the lack of opportunity and rights. It was like something was in the air all over America. Under Golden Frinks' and Small's leadership, we protested for 32 nights. We always began marching from Green Memorial to town hall. We were denied the use of two other churches because the members did not want any backlash. It was a peaceful march. Before we could leave the buildings, some of the members like myself would take any weapons from the marchers, and if any one were suspected of hiding weapons, we would search them. We practiced the non-violence technique. We told people that if they couldn't handle non-violence then they needed to get out. We attended a lot of workshops at Shaw University about conflict resolution.

The town didn't do much. Some of the attacks came from the police. There were around 200 to 300 participants in the marches with about 1,000 people surrounding us calling us names. Some people sprayed us with mosquito repellent and black pepper. That was really hard on me because I had asthma. Those things happen, and we live through them.

One night my car windows were shot out. My dad's car, which was closer to the road, was not touched so I know that this was a planned attack. Also, one night around 2 a.m. we heard bottles being thrown at our tin roof. I talked to the police, but they wouldn't do anything about it. My dad was from a different generation and couldn't understand why we were participating. He would say things like, "I don't want to sit beside a white person," and I would say, "That is not the point."

What were the school boycotts about?

The demonstrators were young people. Some in their 20s and 30s, but most were school age. There was only one couple in their 40s, and that was the deacon of the Green Memorial Church. Small had school-age children that were active in the movement. After the summer of 1963, the students decided to leave school for a march. It was then that I turned on the teachers because they didn't leave the school to help the students. They just stood there in the doorway. *Brown v. Board* was passed in 1954, but it was not acted on. Some blacks made the statement, "The check is written to us, but it hasn't been cashed."

Hecklers would incite violence. One time someone in the crowd stopped the march and told us not to cross a certain line. We stood there in a stalemate. The marchers started praying and eventually we walked back to the church. When we got to the town hall, we would sing and pray. To stop us, they told us we needed a permit to march. It was time to start filling the jails. I didn't go to jail because I had small children at home. We were told not to go in front because you would be jailed. Every consideration was taken to make people aware of the possibilities. We had people who had their heads beat in. We had to explain that they wanted you to respond. The people heckling were white, but even people in our community would criticize me for participating.

What do you remember about Golden Frinks?

Frinks was from Edenton. His wife was a professor at Elizabeth State Teachers College. He went to several areas in the East to help. His direct boss was Martin Luther King, Jr., who visited Windsor, but not Williamston. I can't tell you too much about him. He was raised by a white family who were a major influence on him. When he experienced injustice, it hit him really hard.

Were you a leader in the movement?

I wasn't necessarily a leader, but I was involved. I thought it was a worthy cause. We spent money in the stores, but we couldn't work there, and they would watch us. We couldn't eat in restaurants or stay in hotels. There were still black and white signs up at the courthouse. We had to sit in the balcony of the movie theater.

What role did women play as leaders?

Women are always leaders. If you want a job done well, you get a woman. Men think they have to be aggressive to prove their manhood. Golden Frinks was a leader, but for the most part, men were not willing to take the same chances that women were. Men my husband worked with said they were afraid of losing their jobs. My husband participated and left it up to the Lord to provide. I was only told not to bring the protest to work. I worked odd jobs while I was raising my five children.

Some of the things we fought for got twisted. Sometimes you have to get in the system to change things. I never wanted to be a teacher. I went to college at the age of 33 and got my teaching licensure for K–8th grade. I still really hate teachers because I remember them not responding. I could not take a job in Martin County because I was afraid that I would get a bad placement in response to my participation in the marches. My children were the first group to desegregate their elementary school. I was not worried because I taught them not to respond to violence.

What was your relationship with teachers like?

There were teachers that would call Sarah Small to give her directions. She would tell them that she followed the Lord's direction and if they wanted to give directions that they had to participate. Some supported the movement financially. Teachers were involved but not in a positive way. They were not in the power structure or demonstrating. They tried to stay neutral. Laws had been passed, but the power structure didn't respond. They would close little schools, and built a large school to pacify us. Our protests were not about going to school with white children. It was about getting decent material. Our books were always the hand-me-downs from the white school after they got new books. Also white students would spit on us as they rode past in buses. The idea of consolidating black schools hurt the community. My children went to Rogers Elementary that didn't have as educated a staff as the school they originally went to. I talked to Superintendent Gene Rogers about it, and he said he would not send his children to Rogers. That is when I decided to move. My daughter and son went to school where there were the only three black students in the 3rd grade. They were put in separate classrooms with all white students.

There was one instance during a history lesson. In the history book there was a picture of black people picking cotton, and all the white students started to snicker. I told the teacher to stop using that book, and it was replaced the next year. When children are raised a certain way, it does not matter what is going on.

William Earl Newsome

Black Activist
Interview by Amanda Hilliard Smith
December 28, 2012

What do you remember about the Civil Rights Movement?

Joe Cross was another nice guy. He was a typical good high school boy. He played trombone in the band. I was one year in front of him. He had a brother one year in front of me, and he had a sister who graduated one year in front of my wife. I don't know of any other traits other than being a good guy. That summer he was working in Norfolk, Virginia, as a carpenter. He had experience because his uncle was a renowned carpenter.

At his funeral, I was chosen to be a pallbearer. I was enraged when I found out about his death. I was looking for the truth. It was a hideous situation. I was no different from the average [black] citizen. Even more so when I heard the comments from the Willis's family, I knew there was a red herring flowing up and down someone's river. I think this kind of incident put Williamston on watch. How much of this can you take? It lingered on in the minds of a lot of people, especially the younger folks.

Around the same time there was an argument between L.C. Moore's wife and Mrs. Biggs that led to an altercation. I heard a lot of things that weren't reported in the newspaper, but nothing that would justify murder. At that point you didn't rely on the press. It just seemed that the timing was right for anything.

What do you remember about the protest that took place during the summer of 1963?

The protest in the summer of 1963 was a part of the national thing. It was happening everywhere, especially the South. The spark just fell on us. It brought me to a level. You didn't have news stations; you just had what people wanted you to hear. I didn't need the TV to know there were problems in society.

I was 30 years old; I was married with a son who was one year old. If I wasn't mature, then I would never be mature. Most people in the movement were much younger. They were doing things that other people couldn't do or were afraid to do.

What was Golden Frinks like?

I have often related his tactics to a coach. People might have questioned his methods, but he did what he had to do.

What was Sarah Small like?

The only thing that Sarah Small didn't have was a formal education. She was dedicated to the task, she had guts and she could think. At the end of the day she was right. She exemplified class.

Where you worried about retaliation?

I worked at a life insurance company. My wife worked for the agricultural extension. My contributions to the movement were behind the scenes. I posted bonds for people in jail. The ministers from Massachusetts frequented my house.

The N.C. Fund had an appropriation for community development. Howard Fuller directed the program. The program had college kids from Fayetteville State, NC A&T, and Duke participate. The students stayed in Williamston three months from June to August 1965. Sarah Lynn Wood was graduating from Duke. I apparently wasn't too afraid of retribution to let a white girl stay at my house.

The only retaliation that I saw wasn't about my family. I remember the KKK shooting at the Harris house. I always wondered why they didn't shoot mine up. I was more fearful for my son and wife than for me. I did more of a support role.

Why did you decide to become involved with the board of elections?

Martin Luther King, Jr., died in April 1968, and I had just filed for a position on the Board of Elections. That same year I was doing a lot of voting registration. We went to parts of the county where registration was poor. I first registered in 1961; the register looked down on me. We had six [black] people to run for office in 1968. I was one of them. Two people running for county commissioners, two for board of election, one for register of deeds and Ms. Small for first congressional district. It wasn't just restricted to Martin County. Sarah made a good showing. She carried the message well. It could have been harder on her but she had a support group. We had a coalition that met often. We had the same spirit, but we were all defeated. We were running for a cause. There had to be a first. There was not showboating time. We had a cause in mind.

William J. Morris—county commissioner
Jephro James—county commissioner
Earl Newsome—board of elections
Andrew Pierce—board of elections
Alberta Smith—register of deeds
Sarah Small—First Congressional District

One man was working in the public school system. I was working at Weyerhaeuser at the time as a technician. The boys gave me a hard time. That didn't deter me at all. We didn't know the word retribution. We did what we had to do. My family supported me 110 percent. No one pushed me to participate. It was just me. I had a yearning for fairness.

I have been involved in politics since 1975. I don't take the credit because the system has allowed it. I get satisfaction in seeing it from when it was nothing to where it is now. In the First Congressional District we have eight black sheriffs. It is not black and white. It is about pure fairness. You want to see the numbers going upward. I don't want to see the glitches but it is a part of growth.

Alma and Bob Purvis

Black Activists
Interview by Amanda Hilliard Smith
July 29, 2011

What do you remember about the Williamston Freedom Movement?

Alma Purvis: I remember how the community came together, especially in the area that I lived which is called "down the hill." People were so ready for change that they were willing to risk reprisal. They didn't fear for their lives but jobs. Some of our people worked for white people as maids or whatever. I think the older generations was so determined that their children were going to have a better life. I remember being excited about being in a group of multiple generations. There was something for everyone to do. Everyone had their hand on the plow.

Bob Purvis: I was born in Williamston. I was mostly recruited by Sarah Small. Ms. Sarah lived in the house behind my house; there was a cornfield between our houses. Ms. Sarah's involvement got all of us involved. It was something that gave us ownership to the movement. There were so many people like my mother that worked for white families at that time as a domestic. I had an aunt who worked at different establishments cooking. But they still supported us in what we were doing. There was always encouragement. People who felt they couldn't do anything sent money or food. People did the things that the black community had always done when they saw people doing something that was worthwhile. Ms. Sarah got the ball rolling.

Alma: I remember going to jail. It was both fun and traumatic. I went to jail four times. Once my mother and my two sisters were all in jail; Dad said someone had to cook so we sent Mom out. While we were in jail, we sang songs and we prayed. We were packed in like sardines. There was just such a wonderful feeling like we were accomplishing something. Going to jail got to be a way that you were making a contribution. At that time, we were too young to be charged as criminals, but we were worried that we were going to have criminal records. We grew up believing you had the responsibility to make it better for the next generation. That was the mind set of the community; you were not free just to think about yourself. That was drilled into us from the time I can remember. It is not about you; it is about your people.

Bob: Teachers were great encouragers of that. They would match you up with 2–3 kids to help them. It was something that they knew was necessary for everyone to succeed. There was no such thing as a non-college curriculum or tracking. You had to have Negro history to graduate from high school that was a personal requirement from our principal. He said that you need to know your own history. We were pushed to succeed despite what the circumstances were.

What was E.J. Hayes like?

Bob: It was an all black school. My senior class was 125 students. The high school building is still there. Today we wonder how all these kids got into the classrooms. It was a very nurturing environment. They always knew you could do better. You chose the classes you would have for the next year. When you would go to school, you would have algebra, physics, etc. They would say try it for six weeks and if you were really struggling then we would change it to something else. When you went back they would tell you that you did okay and that you needed to finish the class.

Alma: They assessed your gifts and tried to channel you in the direction that they thought was best for you. They had a vested interest in your future. We had everything in our schools. We had devotion in the morning. We didn't acknowledge that kids with LD [learning disabilities] couldn't learn. They just thought you had to work extra hard. They made you do it, and whatever they had to do to help you they would. Failure wasn't an option. Very few people dropped out of school.

Bob: Finishing school was important. You had teachers like Mr. Bennard, who would take time to read to us one of Langston Hughes' poems. Give us insight into blacks who were talented and were poets, too. Even though we were learning a lot of the English poets, he also introduced us to black writers. My senior year they gave us a senior day off. I couldn't explain to my mom that we were such big people that we got the day off. Probably three-fourths of the kids ended up in the school that day because they could not explain to their parents either. When I got to school, the teachers gave us assignments. They were adamant about being good teachers and seeing that their students did well.

Alma: We were taught everything. They taught us social graces, how to dress, how to carry yourself, self-esteem. Girls that got pregnant disappeared, and then they came back. We were culturally enriched because our teachers were our role models. I grew up wanting to be a teacher. I held them in such high esteem. They were very inspiring just because of who they were and what they did for us.

Bob: Mr. Blackly told me I was smartest kid in 8th grade. You are talking about a kid that didn't think he was going to make it out of the first grade. I looked at my transcript, and I don't know how I made it. I think the greatest thing is the teachers believing in you. They encouraged us and made us do things we didn't want to do. Many of them lived in our community. They would invite themselves to dinner if they thought it was necessary.

Alma: A lot of teachers lived out of town. They were not from Williamston so they would come and stay a week or month. They were very much a part of the community. Our parents didn't come to school, but matters were resolved when parents were called. There were no serious behavior problems. The parents were in total support of the school. Church, school, and community all worked hand in hand with each other. There was no divisions between those institutions. Church did school kinds of things as well. Community people looked after each other's children. That is why when the Civil Rights Movement started, the whole community rallied around it. It was like together we stand and together we fall. We had always had that kind of thinking. We couldn't afford to be divided because we had too many forces coming against us.

Bob: My junior and senior year I worked for the local black doctor, Dr. Wynn, driving and cleaning his office. Being the only black doctor, he had to treat all black people. He was a wonderful man. He and I were like friends instead of employer and employee.

Alma: We had such high respect for teachers and elders. I guess if Ms. Sarah and Golden Frinks had asked us to jump into the Roanoke River, we probably would have. I didn't want to go to Williamston High School because I loved E.J. Hayes. You felt safe and affirmed there. To leave that situation and go to a hostile all white situation was traumatic for me. We were chosen because of the whole non-violence part of the Civil Rights Movement. SCLC foundation was non-violent. They tried to select students that they thought could handle the mistreatment and still be non-violent. You still had to function as a student in that environment; you had to prove to the white establishment that our kids are smart and could compete with anyone else. We were hand-selected. Some others were selected, but they didn't want to go. We weren't the only ones with the opportunity, but they chose not to go. When the elders said you had the type of knowledge and spirit that would serve the community, you don't say no to that. It wasn't that I was so committed. I did it because elders said you are the one. They were there; they were supportive. They had a built-in situation where after we attended school, every day, we would come together so we would have a way to express what we were going through. They would build us back up before we had to go back to school. They didn't just throw us in there and leave us.

We had lots of issues because we were there before complete desegregation. We had assigned seats where we were supposed to sit in the cafeteria. We decided that we wouldn't be regulated to one or two tables for lunch. We started moving around, and there was all kinds of uproar. They threatened to suspend us. We went back and told Mr. Frinks and Mrs. Sarah. They stepped in and took it from there. We didn't have to argue with the principal. When we felt like we were being treated unfairly, they would negotiate. They said your focus is studies, we will take care of everything else, and they did.

Bob: I remember the senior year. We outscored Williamston High School on the SAT and the superintendent came to our principal and said we must have cheated. He wanted us to take the test over again, but the principal refused. The leadership had to stand their ground for what was right even though a lot of them suffered for things like that. They took away baseball as punishment.

Alma: When they assigned us to classes at Williamston, they made sure that they kept us separated. My friend and I were the only two black seniors, we had no classes together. They did the same thing with other students from first grade on up. They didn't want us to feel empowered. They kept us isolated the whole day.

Students were civil; some were savages. They didn't openly embrace us, but they were kind. There was one girl who went out of her way to be nice. Marianne Summerlynn came to me the first day of school and said she was glad I was here. She said, "I hope that I would live to see this day." She walked with me to school, and they threw rocks at us and called her a "nigger lover." She suffered a lot as a result of befriending me. Annett Armstrong Lanier was the other black senior. Her husband, Richard Lanier, was the star football player.

There were other people who were very nice and kind to us. Some would move when I would sit near them in class. In the auditorium, if I was in line, they would go three people ahead not to sit beside me. You could tell that the students who didn't go out of their way to be mean didn't have a problem with your presence.

Was everyone committed to non-violence?

Alma: There were times when we saw some people beat up badly. We couldn't let people get beat up. There were times when people were ready to take up arms and retaliate. That never really happened, but people did get angry about the unnecessary violence. Especially some of the men; my husband got arrested quite a bit.

Bob: I ended up going to Boston early because my nature wasn't non-violent. Being so close to Mr. Frinks and a part of the transportation committee made me a target. One of our biggest fundraisers was juke joints. Ella Mae Ormond owned a café and was part owner of Club Ebony. She knew a lot of the other people in the same business; it was my job to drive her and Mr. Frinks to these businesses. People would give us money. She paid for the buses so that people could attend the March on Washington.

If the law enforcement saw me walking down the street, then I would get arrested. They knew me. The sheriff was a young guy; he wasn't too much older than I was. He had a deputy on his staff that was provoked by the idea that black people wanted freedom. He would go into a frenzy. He would do most of the beating. He would be the initial one to start the violence.

The first time, I was arrested by myself. The other times we were singing songs and playing cards just having a good time. But when you had to go by yourself, it was different. I told the sheriff that this wasn't a place for anyone.

Alma: We called the jailer Uncle Roy. His wife made good biscuits, but we were scared to eat the food. We drove him crazy. We would rattle the cells and make noise all night long. That was fun.

Bob: The sheriff called a few people and got me out. A lot of the time, you would get arrested, and no one would know you were there. He could have just ignored it.

Alma: Bob went "down the hill" to see me. He shouldn't been "down the hill." On the way back he got arrested. Black folks were not supposed to be walking the streets at that time of the night. There wasn't a curfew, but they would assume you were getting ready to march. They created their own curfew.

We would gather at the church and have a worship service and then we would line up. We would march up to the town hall area. Sometimes we didn't make it that far because they would hold us back. That is when we would have to run back to the church. We were always orderly, but we did block the street.

We did a sit-in at Leggett's Drug Store at the soda fountain. They used to have those stools where you could sit and order the sodas. Mr. Leggett was the best decision-maker. He wasn't about to give up black business so he took the stools out so everyone had to stand up. He took the booths and stools out that he had.

What was Green Memorial like?

Alma: Green Memorial was always up for the community. It has always been a church that reached out to help people. It was always open for the people in the area. We didn't lock the doors until the movement started. It was always a safe haven. It wasn't just people "down the hill," but it was well attended by people all over Martin County. Thankfully the pastors believe it was what God wanted them to do. It wasn't just a place that they had church on Sunday. I am thankful that social gospel was a part of church. People always tried to do good things on earth. I am grateful that I have always been a part of that kind of church.

Bob: There where a lot of tent meetings. I don't remember them because I got involved later. There was never anything about denominations. We went to all the churches in the community. My parents were Baptist, but I became a Methodist at age 12. Most of my sisters and brothers became Methodist because we got out of church sometimes on Sunday. It was almost a requirement that when you became 13, you would become a Sunday school teacher. It was focused on the kids.

What was the atmosphere of the march like?

Bob: People on the side would be throwing things or pushing people. There was a lot of physical contact that the police allowed, but as soon as a dispute would break out they would end the march. The police would arrest us. We either got to where we were going to march or sometimes we would show up at town hall. We would come from different angles and formed the group there.

Alma: Whenever they came to arrest us we would sit down. They would have to carry us. Sometimes it was scary. It was frightening. That is why we had the church service before, to give you the courage to endure. I can remember as a child being scared. I was wondering if someone would get seriously hurt. A couple of times we saw people get seriously hurt. One night they hit Tommy Bond with nightsticks. We could hear the crack when it hit his head. The blood was just gushing everywhere. That was very frightening. We cried. They beat Arthur Leary. He almost went into a coma. They pushed us so hard, even children. One time they started shoving us. At the post office, they had iron stakes in a fence around the building. I got pushed and fell on an iron stake. I still have trouble with my stomach to this day. I ended up having to go to the doctor. It didn't take all that force. It was scary but didn't deter us. We would go back and talk about what we could do to prevent provoking them. Every time we would march we would come back and assess and evaluate. Some people were taken out of the march because they put the whole thing in jeopardy. Some people were asked not to march because they felt they didn't have the ability.

Bob: Some black people were within the crowds to keep back protestors. Some of them guys were not allowed to march. Without debriefing some of us would have been deeply scared and would have figured out other methods that weren't non-violent. There was a constant talk about our purpose and why we were there.

Someone talked back to the deputy sheriff in the magistrate's office. He hit everyone who was near him. That deputy lost it every time he was out in the crowd. I have never been to one where he didn't hit someone. I think that was his whole intent that someone was going to get hurt.

Do you remember protesting at E.J. Hayes?

Alma: I remember one time we led a walk out from E.J. Hayes. Jackie Bond did lead that one. The teachers didn't want us to do that. It wasn't a long-range plan. All our supplies came from the white school. Our books were always marked and our books were scratched up or whatever. As students we wanted equal materials and supplies. Since everyone couldn't go to Williamston High School, we deserved to have the same materials. The walk out was staged to say we are tired of getting your second-hand materials. We want our own.

Bob: There was an incident about toilet paper. We were out of toilet paper at the school. Mr. Biggs and Mr. McDonald went to the facilities building and were told that they were out of toilet paper. We thought everyone was out of toilet paper so we were told to bring magazines and newspapers to school. Mr. Biggs heard that a shipment came in so he went back to get the toilet paper. He saw a room with all this toilet paper. When he asked, he was told that this wasn't the toilet paper for the black school. Your paper is made out of a different, coarser type of paper. We didn't know that we weren't given the same toilet paper.

Negro history class had only 15 books for everyone. You couldn't take the book home because they used it in different periods.

Alma: They certainly didn't teach Negro history at Williamston High School. When I went to WHS I thought I would have to take Negro history my senior year. At WHS they looked at me like I was crazy when I asked. That wasn't one of their history courses. I regretted not having the most famous 12th grade English teacher in all of Martin County, Ms. Macadores, the epitome of culture and grace. Whatever good you had in you, she was the one who was going to bring it out. She was the woman who put the finishing touches on you. We were all afraid of her because she had such high standards. You knew when you finished that course, you were going to know something.

Bob: Boys would take home economics classes so they would cook and invite people for lunch. E.J. Hayes didn't have a lunch room until my senior year. Mary Mobley was one of the cooks. When I scored a lot of points in basketball, I would get some extra pieces of chicken or something.

What do you remember about Coach Herman Boone?

Bob: He was my coach both junior and senior year. Senior year he focused on basketball, but after that, he concentrated on football. His 1960s teams were the best in the state. Ricky Lanier was starting defensive linebacker for UNC-Chapel Hill. Cleo "Happy Jack" Whitaker scored 24 touchdowns in 6 games, fastest guy in the state. He was probably Boone's greatest player.

Coach was a regular guy who played pick-up games with us, teachers versus students. He would come to the house and talk to us. All of the coaches were teachers; you weren't going to get by because of athletics. They were not going to let you neglect your academics for sports. If you wanted to go to a college, when you left E.J. Hayes academically you were eligible.

Alma: He was friendly and warm. He was tough; he didn't play.

Bob: Coach told you what he thought you could do. He told you if he didn't think that you were living up to your potential. He was an in-your-face kind of coach.

What role did teachers play in the movement?

Bob: Teachers' jobs were in jeopardy. Teachers encouraged us. Teachers saw danger in marching from the fire trucks and dogs. It was reminiscent of what you saw in Alabama. We were so determined that they couldn't stop us. We didn't get far before they got us. Not even a half of block from the school.

Alma: When we marched the children were in the center. Men were on the outside, where they took the brunt of the violence. The teachers were concerned that there wouldn't be any adults to shelter us from whatever violence might come.

Bob: They had been doing a wonderful job for all those years, and it was just one day they couldn't get us to listen. We were not about to listen; this was ours.

What was Frinks like?

Alma: I got to speak at his funeral. All I could think about was, "What a man, what a man." Mr. Frinks was the bomb. He was fun. As a young person, you couldn't get enough of Mr. Frinks. He was young at heart, he laughed a lot. When he talked, you would hang on every word. You could feel something emanating from him when he spoke. He was passionate. He loved everyone. He was handsome and powerful. What attracted me to him was that white people feared him. There was finally someone black that white people feared like a monster. They hated him but feared him. I probably had a savior complex.

Bob: He was everyone's mentor. He gave you the truth about the way it was. How we were responsible for making these changes. If something is going to happen, then you are going to have to be the one to make it happen. He took our opinions seriously.

Alma: He had a lot of confidence in us. We were youth leaders. He gave us a lot of responsibilities, and he was proud of us. He brought us to the front of the church and talked about how well we did. He was excellent at building your self-esteem. He saw your gifts and talents. He was very respectful and never talked down to us. When we raised concerns, he listened and took into account what we said. Then he made some changes.

Bob: Sarah Small brought the spiritual aspect to everything. Sarah Small kept Frinks grounded. He was a guy who would take a lot of chances. Sarah would always pray about it. My time with him was always enjoyable. He would stay 2 to 3 days, and I would drive him home because he was too tired. On the long drive home, he would talk about his day. We were afraid to let him go home alone.

He knew everyone; if he didn't know them then he acted like he knew them. I told you about all the people he would see for fundraising. He left with the funds. He made sure they understood that the money was used for the cause. I still don't know where the money for the Florida trip came from.

Alma: He was a tremendous community organizer. We met every night and the church was full every night. Whatever Sarah Small and he came up with as far as strategies, they got support. People felt like Golden Frinks had your back. He is going to get you a lawyer, get you out of trouble. He is going to be there for you, whatever. People trusted him with their wives and children. My mother loved him. He bridged the gaps between all the generations.

It was a sacrifice because the SCLC couldn't pay him for all the time he put into it. I know he didn't get compensated. He spent a lot of his own money. He would take youth leaders out for fun. We could goof off and have some fun. He felt it was necessary that we have a normal life as well. We got to act like normal kids.

Bob: He made sure we went to the March on Washington and to the first SCLC Conference in Richmond. Frinks had to find transportation and housing. He took as many people as he could. My grandmother and them even went to Florida. My grandmother, Ora Clemones, was a special person. She knew there was going to be a day. I think it was the same way the slaves saw it, that despite of all the hardships, there was going to be a day that was going to better for their children.

Alma: A lot of the women "down the hill" served as cooks and watched over the church. Vinnie Hodges served as SCLC secretary. She was a beautiful lady, tall and just beautiful. She did a lot of the driving, too.

Bob: Frinks got me a job in Collins Department Store. I was hired as a stock boy, but Frinks told me to tell the owner that if he hired me as a clerk the movement would lift the boycott on the store. The owner told me that he would lose the white customers. The store was about to go into foreclosure and Mayor Green bought the business. Mayor Green became rich at the end of the boycott. The mayor bought all the businesses about to be foreclosed on. He went to the bank and bought them all up. He never said anything against us. He just kept quiet; he saw where he was going to be at the very end. He didn't wait; when someone went out of business he would buy it. He really made out after the boycott. He owned most of Williamston.

What was the Freedom Choir?

Bob: The choir was formed right when the movement got started. In 1964 we travelled to Vermont and Massachusetts. The Reverend LeGarge played the piano like Jerry Lee Lewis. Ministers would come in from different churches outside of Martin County to preach. The

Freedom Choir took a lot of Christian songs and changed the words. Some of the songs came from other civil rights movements.

What was Sarah Small like?

Alma: I want to talk about how wonderful Sarah Small and Golden Frinks were. They were our mother, father, spiritual leader, advisor, and counselor. They were awesome. Fortunately Sarah Small went to Massachusetts. When the nuns and ministers from Massachusetts came to march with us, many stayed with us. Five, I think. They told my mom that if she let me go to Massachusetts they would pay for my schooling. I went to stay with Father Finley, an Episcopal priest, and his wife. There were several other ministers, Father Harmon, and Roger McDonald.

I remember going to Vermont and staying with the Reverend McDonald and working at a summer camp. I didn't see another black person all summer. When I got there, his son said, "You're dirty; you got to take a bath." I agreed because I had just ridden from North Carolina to Massachusetts. I took a bath. When I got back, he said, "You are still dirty." His son had never seen a black person before. His father apologized and said I was the first black person his son had ever seen. He didn't know what to make of it.

I left in 1965. The day after I graduated I was on my way to Massachusetts. There was nothing for me in Williamston, no jobs. We had such a wonderful network of people in Massachusetts. I stayed with Father Finley and his family. I worked as a secretary at his church, St. Ann Episcopal Church. It was where we got married. I was a part of the largest black class at my college; there were 15 black students. I went back into the same situation; it was different, but there was still racism there. We continued the Civil Rights Movement when we went to Massachusetts. Sarah Small worked at Packard Manse. We use to go there to be around her.

Marie Robertson

White Teacher
Interview by Amanda Hilliard Smith
October 7, 2005

What happened in Williamston during desegregation?

When it first began we had demonstrations and marches. That was really unnerving to white people. The togetherness of black people was something that they were not accustomed to. The community had gotten along in the way people did a long time ago. The blacks stayed here and the whites stayed there. We played with blacks, but there was no social organization. When it started there was a lot of unrest. My mother, Lillian Peele, was very in tune to the Civil Rights Movement, and she lost a lot of her white friends because of it. She knew that it was coming and that we needed to learn how to get along. It was very hard for others to take. It made it difficult on her two daughters. What she was saying was very true, that they were people just like we are. I remember when I was teaching school, she told me that one day a black would be my boss. She was right.

The scariest thing that happened in relation to integration was in 1965. I was teaching 7th grade and had three black children in my classroom. One white boy was late getting to school the first day, and there were no desks left. When he came in, he wanted one of the blacks to get up and give him a seat. That was what they were accustomed to. Of course, I didn't make the black students move. The mother called outraged about what happened at school. At the end of the first day of integration, I looked out at the street and saw a line of whites lined up across the street waiting for school to be out. We had police and firemen on campus with riot gear on. That was the most frightening thing of the whole experience. Nothing ever happened, but the fact that they were there, the intimidation was traumatic for me. Once we got started, we didn't have many problems because there were only a limited number of blacks.

Then Martin County had to have teachers to start crossing the racial lines. At the time my husband was assistant superintendent, and the first thing a lot of the white teachers wanted to know was where Marie was going to go. I was among the first to cross the racial lines. I was sent to Rodgers school with two other white teachers. I thought I was going to teach the 7th grade but they needed a third grade teacher. I decide that I could teach 3rd grade. When I went into the classroom with all little black faces, they told me that I would not have any textbooks until after the first six weeks. Those little children were just as eager to learn as anybody was. After that, the majority of my teaching career has been working with blacks.

As far as the integration period, it went smoothly at Rodgers since it is a country school. It was a historically black school, but it was fully integrated after they started drawing districts.

What kind of relationship did you have with the parents and black community?

The parents were very good. I can relate because my mother had letters written to her from black parents saying, "Mrs. Peele, we want our children to have a good education. Can you help us get some good teachers?" Black parents were interested in their children and wanted the best for their children. They were very cooperative and easy to work with.

What is the biggest factor for desegregation in this area?

I think it was more from the federal government and the threats of losing your federal funds. This is a poor county, and we depend a great deal on that. We had some strong black leaders, but I was not involved with that.

How did the loss of funds affect your husband, who was the assistant superintendent?

He worked with the Title I programs of the Elementary Secondary Education Act (ESEA). That was where all the federal money was coming from. I remember in the 1968–69 school year, they cut off our federal funds because they were not being spent correctly. My husband's salary stopped for a month while they were figuring it out.

I made some really dear friends there, and I was accepted. I was frightened at first because I was not accustomed to the makeup of the school. Within a month, I just didn't see the color. It got to a place where it would surprise me to see a white child in a class. During integration, there wasn't a lot of interaction between the races. Fortunately we had a lot of teachers that were skilled in handling any problems that would come up between the races. At the school, I felt I was an outsider mostly because of my work with the federal programs.

Richard Eugene Rogers

Superintendent of Schools
Interview by Amanda Hilliard Smith
October 9, 2005

What happened in Williamston during the desegregation of public schools?

I was aware of the Civil Rights Act and *Brown vs. Board.* I knew that schools had to be desegregated. There was no way to get out of that, while the general population didn't appear to be ready for it. The public felt like they could sidestep it before it would become a reality. I think our school board was sensitive to it and aware it would take place. They were between a rock and a hard place because of their constituents. They were mindful of the fact that it was going to happen.

Until the time came for action, I don't think people were fully aware, except for the black marches. But that was only about a year before we had to start breaking down the system. When blacks marched, there were whites present, but it is my understanding that there were plenty of police to keep it in balance.

I moved my family back here in the summer of 1964. I only recall one march that took place after Martin Luther King, Jr.'s, assassination, but several took place prior. I took part in the march with the mayor of the town, members of the school board, county commissioners, and local ministers on a Sunday afternoon. The march was from Hayes School to the baseball field. The dignitaries sat on the platform. Sarah Small was the leader, and we sang songs like "We Shall Overcome." So that was what occurred before we got down to the hard job of actually exchanging students from one school to another.

The beginning of desegregation was on a voluntary basis with 12 black students being transferred to white schools. We just eased into it from that point on, just took one step at a time. It was obvious at the time that this wasn't the finished plan.

It was the black leaders that sent their children to Williamston High School. I believe that some blacks were not any more interested in desegregation than whites. It wasn't a large number of blacks that wanted desegregation. They were comfortable where they were, not that they weren't sympathetic to bettering their situation.

What was it like being a superintendent at that time?

Lots of pressure; I never had a cross burned in my yard, but I did receive threatening phone calls from the white community.

We started to force integration by pairing schools. Pairing schools took place in districts. We paired the black and white schools in each district and forced them all to go to the same school. In all cases the black high school students went to the white high school. It was a fool proof way of doing it. We had to draw solid district lines. As far as I can recall, there were no requests for transfers out of those districts. It was a pretty tense time. I lived in Williamston, so I know more of what happened in that area. I know that there were whites that observed the marches. Of course, they were concerned, but I don't know their motives. It was a pretty tight time.

The white community had three or four months to prepare for it [desegregation]. The white community had grown to accept it except for a few diehards. I think there was enough time that it was an easy enough transition.

We had been negotiating with Health, Education, and Welfare (HEW) all along. We tried a couple of things with bond issues, but consolidation was the issue. Those bond issues failed, of course. So we had to make do with the schools we had.

From that point on, we had three years where we had non-violent sit-in incidents in the school. One morning in Williamston High School, all the black students sat down in the auditorium. Mr. Farnell, the principal, convinced them that they had to go to class. I never understood why they boycotted other than to show their strength in hopes of influencing policy. I don't recall any change that came about because of it.

In Robersonville, there was a sit-in in the hallways. When I got there, we got them into the auditorium to talk to them about what they wanted. The issues were not unreasonable, and we accommodated whatever we could. On one occasion, the buses ran and no one got on throughout the county. The other incidents did not happen at the same time so this was the first countywide effort. There was no issue that I could determine. From time to time, the black leadership would meet with me. Sometimes voices were raised, but there were no standoffs.

Going back to Freedom of Choice, one of the jobs we had to do was prepare forms and send them to every student to see if they wanted to change schools. Only about 12 responded, and those 12 stayed the whole time. I don't recall any particular incidents.

This happened at a bad time. Mr. Farnell at the beginning of the year changed the valedictorian to an honors group. There was a protest because the valedictorian was supposed to be a black student. There was no real big protest or anything. He was honored and there were no ulterior motives to set aside James Smith.

After three or five years, things smoothed out. There were a handful of whites that never accepted it, but most went along with it. I would say that athletics was the biggest factor in bringing the two races together. We formed a transition team to work on symbols. In Williamston they took the white school's colors and the black school's mascot of a tiger. That turned out really well.

What were in your opinion the major factors in seeing desegregation enforced in Williamston?

We got our pressure from Washington, D.C. The state had some laws on the books that put off desegregation. Several of the surrounding systems were desegregated through a lawsuit. Frankly, our board would have appreciated a lawsuit because it would have taken the pressure off them. Washington's threat to federal funding really dictated what we had to do. In the late '50s Congress passed the ESEA (Elementary Secondary Education Act) that put a lot of money into the school system. Once you had used that money for a couple of years, you grew accustomed to it. If you took it out, you got a big hole in your budget that you had to figure out how to cover.

Our board was against the wall. I don't recall a single board member that was racist, but representing the white constituents, they had to put forth the defense. When it finally came, they were all on board.

At least four years after the initial freedom of choice, the school board got legislation to expand its board to include a black member. It was a gesture that they thought they needed to make. When the voting rights legislation passed, they redistricted so that blacks would have a better chance in getting elected to the board. It started at five and went to seven. Now it is wide open to who gets elected to the school board.

As superintendent, what was your interaction with HEW (Health, Education, and Welfare)?

HEW could withdraw funds or incite a lawsuit. I never heard of them inciting a lawsuit. HEW representatives, several individuals and one delegation, came to Williamston and offered all kinds of assistance. Then the big delegation came down to discuss pairing of the schools. The delegation was made up of one black person and three white people from all over the nation.

We had one hearing in Washington, D.C., and I don't remember what it was about. We didn't have a plan when we went up there. It was a simulated court that took testimony. Mr. Peel was our attorney. The judge was very frank and basically told us that we must desegregate.

I think everyone thought that with time we would be able to accomplish it. I think the blacks felt that way too and allowed us the time we needed. We had to bite the bullet and prepare the schools for desegregation. It was hard because I had to manage the schools and deal with everything that was going on.

It worked out. We were under pressure. We started with freedom of choice, but once it didn't prove to be effective, we used pairing of the schools. HEW never took the burden off us or offered us any relief. Washington was straightforward, but they did try to accommodate.

Did you have any communication with other school systems?

No, but we knew what was going on. When the other school systems lost their lawsuit, it was good evidence that we weren't going to win a similar suit.

My first year was as assistant superintendent from 1964 to 1965. I became superintendent in the 1965–1966 school year. Superintendent Manning had already announced his retirement a few years before I arrived. He didn't want to stay through the whole episode. He had his 30 years, and it was an opportune time for him to step down.

How did you choose teachers to cross the racial lines?

No teachers volunteered, but we carefully chose teachers that we thought would be accepted. We interviewed the teachers, and we didn't send them against their will.

You mentioned a bus boycott; what happened?

Teachers were allotted based on attendance. We just communicated the fact that we would lose money if the parents didn't send their children to school. We wanted to find out the black community's communication system. The administrative staff followed the school buses during the boycott to make sure that the drivers were stopping and not spreading the message. They were not. I am still puzzled as to how the word got out. They had meetings, but not all the parents went to them. They took place in the middle of the week and that added to the logistics issue. We assumed that it was the churches.

Were black teachers discouraged from participating in the movement?

The blacks were sensitive to the fact that black teachers could be fired. I do not know of a serious incident with a teacher. I think it would have been an extreme case for that to have happened. We didn't have tenure back then, so it could have happened. If that teacher sued us, we would not have had any grounds to dismiss them.

There was a law on the books in North Carolina that put assignment on a local level. It was something that made us think we could avoid desegregation. It didn't, however, deter the federal government from doing anything.

My kids were at Hayes during this time. They would say there were rumors that Black Panthers were coming. It was just a lot of scare tactics.

I was in graduate school during *Brown*, and I wrote an essay about desegregation. I argued that desegregation should start at the first grade and desegregate up one grade each year. You have to give people time to process.

We had some strong black leadership. They were right. I was surprised that they never brought a lawsuit against us because we dragged our feet. Maybe they just wanted to see us do it.

What was your interaction with Golden Frinks?

Frinks was instrumental, but the only real contact I had with him was five or six years after consolidation. He organized a march from Jamesville to Williamston for some issue that I don't even remember. He met with me, and we solved the problem. He was a smart and pleasant sort of person. Sarah Small played a prominent role. She was mostly a motivator, but she did lead some marches. She never appeared before the board.

Ida Small Speller

Black Activist, Daughter of Sarah Small
Interview by Amanda Hilliard Smith
July 13, 2011

What do you remember about the Williamston Freedom Movement?

I was 13 in 1963. I remember one day my brother Jimmie and I were outside playing. Mom asked us if we would like to be in a march. We thought it was a march similar to a parade or something of that nature; we were excited because we were thinking bands and majorettes.

The following day Mom sent us up to a tent to meet with the Rev. David Carter. Carter was the pastor of a particular church that was using a tent before the building was built. When we got there, there were three men and about seven to ten young people including the Reverend Carter's children. We knew the Reverend Carter but the other two men were not known to us. Later we found out their names were Golden Frinks and the Rev. Fred LaGarge from Edenton. We were told that Mr. Frinks worked for Dr. Martin Luther King and the Reverend LaGarge was Mr. Frink's assistant. After the Reverend Carter prayed, Mr. Frinks immediately started telling us what the gathering was all about. He told us it was about equal rights for the Negro; he pointed out how there were signs that stated where we could sit, drink, eat or go. He talked about the injustice of it all and how our marching will turn all of this around. The Reverend LaGarge taught us freedom songs and he played the piano as we sung. He was a skilled musician and would teach us songs with a twist on them.

The first march as I reflect back was like a dry run; none of us really knew exactly what was going to happen or the magnitude of what we were preparing to embark on. I believe that a permit was obtained because we marched right down the middle of the street from Sycamore to Main to city hall. And the police and sheriff departments made sure that traffic was diverted so that we could do the march. My mother was at her best friend's house, Wardell Brown, at the time we passed by Hill Street and she saw us following behind these men as our leaders and she told Wardell she could not allow some people from another town lead our children, so she decided to join us even though she was six weeks pregnant at the time and stepped right to the front with Mr. Frinks, the Reverend LaGarge and the Reverend Carter. As we quietly walked to city hall, there were people on the sidewalks watching us; the blacks were cheering and the whites were jeering. After we got there [to city hall] we prayed and sang "We Shall Overcome" and returned back to the tent.

The next night with more young people joining we did the same thing again, and this went on for about two to three weeks. The group was outgrowing the tent; the leaders started seeking a larger place for us to meet, preferably a church. Every church that was approached denied the movement access because of fear; they saw how churches were being bombed and burned throughout the South for hosting civil rights meetings. My mother played for several churches in the area, but only one that was actually in the town; the others were in the rural areas. It happened that she played for the Junior Choir at Green Memorial; one Saturday after a rehearsal there, she approached William Dorsey Speller, who was the head deacon there, and asked if it would be possible for the movement to meet there; he told her that he would talk with the board of deacons. The rest is history.

We marched a few times before the city ordinance was passed saying we couldn't march without a permit. The first time we marched after getting the permit we marched from "down the hill" to city hall. On our way up the hill after the steps there were a lot of white jeerers standing on sidelines. I remember hearing one lady saying, "Daddy, get yo' gun and shoot the niggas," and him saying, "Ah, hell, I ain't going to jail for no nigga." Once we all had passed them they followed us to city hall; once we got there we sung a few songs and then we kneeled to pray. I can't remember who prayed that night, but the prayer was so powerful that the power of the Holy Spirit visited everyone out there. When I looked up the lady who had coaxed her daddy to get his gun had her hands up in praise; that was a very powerful night. When we marched back to church most of the jeerers had left.

Soon the town denied us the permits. The first time that they denied the permit, Sarah Small informed us that we were going to march anyway; she warned us that we may get arrested and possibly go to jail. The children were very excited about the prospect of going to jail and being a part of the civil disobedience. As we gathered to go to city hall that night, we were met on the way by the police, and we had been told that once they approached us we were to sit where we stood and that we did. This was my first arrest; I didn't know what to expect. They took us to the police station and processed us; those that were 15 and under they released to their parents or guardians. At the time I was 13, but could easily pass for 16, so when they got my information I told them that I was 16. They locked us up in a room similar to a jury room; we had been told that we would be bailed out that same night. One of the girls in the room with us had said that she was 16 as well but she was really 15. She cried the whole time we were there, saying how she wanted to go home, how she wanted to see her boyfriend; I was surprised to see her wimp out like that. We were there for about two or three hours and then we were bailed out. Mr. Styron Bond, Sr., was one of our primary people who bailed us out, along with other homeowners. There was a gentleman from Windsor who owned a lot of land; his name was Tommie Bond. His family would come over to Williamston after working the fields all day and march with us, as well as went to jail.

The next time we went to jail, we didn't get out in hours. We spent the night, but we were well taken care of by Mrs. Hattie Speller who cooked for us; she and others would send us fried chicken, collard greens, cornbread and desserts. Our jailer, who we fondly called Uncle Roy, was a nice person; he was small in stature and his wife cooked for the jail. Uncle Roy would bring us the food that was sent by the ladies from "down the hill" until he was told not to do so anymore; we had to eat what the town provided. Even he said his wife didn't cook as good as the ladies from "down the hill." During one of the lockups the Town of Williamston were getting tired of footing bills that they had not budgeted for, so they decided to try to deter the men from coming back to jail.

According to John Small and Bill Mobley it was in July and they had put approximately 50-some-odd men in an eight-man cell and turned the heat on. Now the story differs a little; John believes that the water that accrued on the floor was from perspiration; he said the men were dehydrating. Bill Mobley said that they turned on the water and stopped up the sinks so that the water would flow so that they could cool off. The water started running downstairs to the ladies' cell and that's when the jailer came up to see what was going on and put the window up so that they could get air. John said that he could hear the sizzling from the radiator, and when they reached out to touch it, it was hot. They both say that they were packed in like sardines.

What do you remember about integrating public facilities?
We went to a number of places to picket, sit-in, and sing. The first place we tried to integrate was the Watts Theatre; Brenda Williams was the first up to the ticket counter on the white side to purchase a ticket. The person who sold the tickets denied her a ticket, and Brenda wanted to know what made her money any different than a white person's. She said it has "In God We Trust" on it, and that George Washington was on her dollar, too. We were told if they did not sell us tickets we were to immediately sit down and block the entrance, which we did, and we were arrested.

Once we got out of jail, the next day we went to the Griffin's Quick Lunch; it was about 30 of us in total. Griffin's had limited seating on the white side so we went in about eight to ten at a time; as they arrested one group another group would go in until we all were locked up. According to John Small the first group was, including himself, Vinnie Hodges, Annette Armstrong Lanier, Alma Freeman Purvis, Jackie Bond Shropshire, Robert Purvis, Clara Goss, Mary Hansome and William Nelson. John said that some of the workers were threatening to hit them with the ketchup bottles and the hot sauce bottles, but the owner told them not to do that because that was what we wanted. After that day the proprietors started locking their doors when they saw us coming so we just stood in front of the establishments and sang.

One night we marched up the hill to the S&V supermarket to sing and pray. The mosquito truck was sent out under the pretense of spraying the mosquitoes and tried to spray us. Miraculously a light wind came and lifted the fog right over our heads and no one coughed or got sick; that was definitely divine protection. That was when Mr. Frinks coined WIAM as being the acronym for Williamston Is A Mess, even though it was the radio station's call letters.

During the day we would picket the various places that would not let us in. When we went to Shamrock to go in for service the owner locked the door. At the time Mrs. Mobley was working there as a cook and when she saw how he treated her people she took off her apron and quit and joined the movement full-time. When we attempted to integrate the swimming pool, they closed it down and did not ever open it again; instead they made it a parking lot. The bowling alley closed before they would let us in. We tried to go into the R&C; they would only serve us through a little hole on the side, and we boycotted them as well. We tried to integrate the Martin General Hospital, but they wouldn't even take our information until we went to the colored side. We went to a few white churches; although they did not call the police or put us out, they treated us very coolly.

Who were the leaders of the Williamston Freedom Movement?

Shortly after the protest at Watts Theatre, the group voted my mother as president of the SCLC. She was 36 years old and pregnant with her last child, Freeda. I don't remember whether we had a vice president or not. Brenda Williams, secretary; Hattie V. Speller, assistant secretary; Levester Harris, treasurer; Annette Lanier, Alma Freeman,

Jackie Bond, William Nelson Williams, Robert Purvis and John Small were the youth leaders; and Ella Mae Ormond was the executive director. Other leaders included Mary L. Mobley, Francis King, Mary Hansome and Vinnie Andrews Hodges and William Nelson.

Do you remember any violence associated with the movement?

One night after we had our meeting at the church—it was on training on non-violence—the door burst open and several came running in and it sounded like guns were being fired and the men looked as though they had been shot with what we thought was blood on heads and arms. It turned out to be a prank by the leaders; they wanted to see our reactions if something like that really happened and to teach us what to do and to be ready for anything. Bill Mobley remembers that one night the police was chasing a fellow by the name of Chinch Brown and he ran straight to the church "down the hill" because he knew that it was a safe haven.

Bill Mobley and John Small remembers how some of the white hecklers or KKK would go around using a device on their trucks to scratch the movement's vehicles, or use an instrument to back into the movement's cars and put holes in their radiators. Some of the guys laid in waiting for the culprits and put an end to it, the way only they know how.

The night the KKK came to our house, they were attempting to burn a cross. Mom turned on all the lights. There was a minister from Harvard Divinity School staying with us. He said, "Why are you turning on the lights? They can see us." She told the minister, "We can see them too." She told the crowd that Halloween was over. She was always skittish, but through the movement she became brave.

One time we were marching up the hill from the church to go to city hall and was stopped by law enforcement; they wouldn't let us come up the steps and we wouldn't go back to the church so we just sat where we stood. It was going to get bloody. They cattle prodded people trying to get them to move, but to no avail. John Small tells the story of how this one guy, Blue Watson, who was a real huge guy, was being cattle prodded and he didn't flinch, and after several attempts at prodding him, the officer thought it wasn't working so he tested on himself, and according to John it almost knocked him out. That was the night that Governor Sanford sent in the National Guard. This ended with a compromise between Sarah Small and Sheriff Rawls; she told him if they would leave then the marchers would go back to the church.

What do you remember about the demonstration at E.J. Hayes?

One day we had planned to march from the school. None of the teachers were involved because they were afraid that their contracts would not be renewed if it was found out that they were part of the movement. That day was a day of no return, as we gathered to march downtown to city hall. As we were approaching the railroad track up from the school, mysteriously, the train came and stopped, blocking the pathway. There were several people up front; Jackie Bond, the Reverend Carter, John Small and others were met with police brutality. Jackie was hit with two prods in her abdominal area, and the prods were so powerful that they knocked her off her feet and she fell to the ground in agony and pain and she was crying for help. The Reverend Carter was also prodded and others.

John Small ran back to Jackie's father's store, who was Styron Bond, Sr., and told him what had happened; meanwhile we were all running back to the school campus, and I noticed people coming out of Mr. Styron's store with sodas. When I went in there to see what was going on he was passing out sodas saying to us to, "Drink the sodas and throw the bottles," and that's what we did.

According to Bill Mobley someone said, "Look, they got Charles Howard." When he looked they had Charles, preparing to put him in the police car, when a couple of fellows threw bricks and hit the officers in the back and they let Charles go to attend their wounds and he got away. Most of the adult leaders, not all, were trying to get us under control and to stop throwing the bricks and bottles. The next thing we knew, the fire truck had arrived and was at the fire hydrant across from the school preparing to hook up the hose to spray us. And again, miraculously the water only came out as a drizzle, not the hard force that they were expecting. God was truly with us that day and throughout the whole Williamston Civil Rights Movement. That scene was an eye-opener to the teachers and the other students; they saw that whether they participated or not they were considered a part of the whole ordeal.

What do you remember about the boycott of local stores?

One of the things we were marching for was the equality in the school system and it was getting close to September and it was time to start buying school clothes. That's when the boycott of all Williamston downtown stores took place. We were told to shop at neighboring towns, such as Windsor, Robersonville, or Washington, and the people with cars formed carpools to make sure that people that did not have transportation could go elsewhere. At the same time we were told to boycott the grocery stores as well and to go to black owned grocery stores or go out of town. These boycotts were very effective, so much so until the town council sent for the leaders from Williamston to hear their demands, the downtown stores suffered tremendously, and it was coming up close to Christmas and they really wanted us to shop with them. However, we were still getting secondhand books from the white school, so we continued to boycott the school, which was Hayes. Of course we did not get 100 percent support but we did it anyway.

What happened when the ministers from Massachusetts visited?

In November of '63, 11 ministers came to Williamston from the North to help us out after consulting with Dr. King as to where they could best help and he told them to go to Williamston. Nine of the ministers were from Massachusetts, one from Philadelphia, and one was from Rutland, Vermont. They were labeled by the Williamston authorities as outside agitators. After getting briefed on what was expected they immediately hit the streets of Williamston, marching with their black brothers and sisters. They were arrested but put into separate cells, the ones that were designated for whites only. According to Henry Byrd, one of the ministers who still is with us said that they shoved them into the cells and took the mattresses off the bunks, which meant that they had to sleep on the bare metal. They decided not to eat until they were put in jail with their black brothers. After it made the news that they were on a hunger strike for this cause, they were eventually put in the cells with the blacks.

When the ministers went back to their respective homes they

started a campaign to get funding to bring the Williamston Freedom Choir up north along with some of their leaders. When we found out we were going to Boston everyone was ready to jump on the bandwagon. In December of '63, two buses left Williamston for the North. Our first stop was Philadelphia, the home of one of the ministers whose name was Paul Stagg; we stayed overnight and moved on to Massachusetts. Our first stop was in Roxbury at the home of John Harmon, who was another minister that had come to Williamston. Sadly, Father Harmon died last year.

We stayed in Stoughton, Massachusetts, the bulk of the time that we were there at a place called Packard Manse. Packard Manse was huge place with several houses surrounding it. The main building was used for retreats and campers, so there was plenty of room for all of us, which numbered to about 80. It was more along the lines of a university dorm. There was a huge dining area and kitchen where our meals were prepared. We visited various churches and sung; we also marched in Roxbury. While we were there they asked one of the young people to speak and Barbara Smith was chosen, and one of the things I remember her saying was the North needed to clean up their own backyard before trying to come and clean others. That went over big. At the time I didn't understand that statement, but boy, do I ever get it now. We went to the home of Henry Byrd, one of the ministers that came to Williamston, which was on Martha's Vineyard; we also went to Vineyard Haven, Tisbury and Oak Bluffs and at each place the Freedom Choir sang. Then we went to Rutland, Vermont, to another minister's church, I can't recall his name.

We had a wonderful experience; we met Virgil Woods who was a known civil rights leader in the Boston area. We had a litany of freedom songs and we had dynamite harmony. We sung songs like "I'm Gonna March into Williamston in the Morning, Lord"; "Ole Freedom"; "Give Me That Old Time Freedom"; "If You Miss Me"; "I Ain't Gonna Let Nobody Turn Me Around"; "Farther on Up the Road"; "I Shall Not Be Moved"; "There Will Be Freedom in Williamston"; "I'll Overcome"; and "We Shall Overcome," just to name a few. We were up north approximately nine to ten days, I believe. We came back to Williamston revived and had such an incredible time that we shared with those that did not get a chance to go.

We continued to work in the movement. We were asked to come to Danville, Virginia, where James Bevel asked us to sing at a church. We were asked by Dr. King to come to St. Augustine, Florida, to help them out in their civil rights struggle. A busload of us from Williamston went to Florida. We were all excited to be going there; some of us had never been to Florida before, just like we had never been to Massachusetts or Vermont before.

Williamston was a town where everyone knew everyone else. We didn't realize how good we had it in Williamston until we got to Florida. We got to Florida that morning and marched that night. We were met with dogs, KKK, Billy clubs, cattle prods and a group of angry law enforcement and Floridians. The following day we were assigned to different places to go to try and integrate; my group went to the Fountain of Youth, which was founded by Ponce de Leon. When they would not admit us, we were arrested. When the authorities found out we were not from the area, they decided that even though we were too young to be put in with the adults, they detained us in the local jail until our parents or guardians came and signed us out.

There were 30 people placed in a jail cell meant for only 6 people. We were put in a cell that was meant for about six people, which meant most of us had to sleep on the floor; we only had one toilet in the stall and one small sink. To really add insult to injury they fed us baby food for the whole seven days. Although my mother was there and could have signed me out, she chose not to; she thought it would be unfair to the others from Williamston if she took me out. I didn't know that until we got out, or I would have figured out something. I didn't know that they got bailed out after a day or so in the Jacksonville Penitentiary. I am not sure of all the people from Williamston that went but I remember Sarah Small, Mary Mobley, Levester Harris, Mrs. Dickens, Ollie and Bill Mobley, Eulah Purvis Rodgers, Annette Armstrong Lanier, eight Ball (William Frank Williams), Robert Earl Purvis, Daryl Hargett, Audrine Scott, Vinnie Hodges, and about 20 others that I don't remember right off hand. All I know is when I left Florida, I promised the Lord and anybody that would listen I would never go to jail again, and I didn't. I was cured.

Did you take part in Freedom of Choice in the schools?

I didn't have freedom of choice; my mother sent me. I was in eighth grade. Most of the teachers were hostile toward us. If they had refuge in their teacher, then the kids wouldn't be so bad. Our parents didn't walk us to school even the first day. Whites lined the walkway and heckled us. There were some kids that they got physical with. I didn't see it but I was told James Smith was attacked quite often.

I only went the first year because my brother needed a babysitter. I went to Massachusetts to live with him. My brother got the connection with the ministers who came down to help us in 1963. He was 21 and newly married. He lost his job because of the movement. He contacted Paul Chapman, who told him that he would help him get a job. I came back in 1967 and then I went back to Boston to finish school. The entire family left for Boston—all five siblings.

How would you describe your mom?

She was a very spiritual person. She had deep faith and everything she did she prayed first. She had very strong leadership skills. She came to Massachusetts to run an economic house and got a job at University of Massachusetts as a chaplain. She never received religious training but she had so much experience working with young people.

She eventually got on the SCLC's pay roll. Frinks started a group called CARCAMP. It was supportive of prisoners and helping them get back into society. It was just in the Boston area.

Ruth Mobley Spruill and Ollie Mobley Marshal

Black Activists, Daughters of Mary Mobley
Interview by Amanda Hilliard Smith
July 9, 2011

What do you remember about the Williamston Freedom Movement?
Ruth Spruill: In 1966, I attended first grade at Church Street School.

The three Harris children and I were the only black students. Blondell was among the first five black students to graduate from Williamston. We would catch a cab to school. We didn't have a car during that time. We would have to wait for Mr. Robert Blan to pick us up. Children learn behavior from adults. We got along with the white kids. There were some who wouldn't play with you. I remember one boy sitting behind me and pulling my ponytail all the time. In third grade we played tag. The principal [Ruth Manning] told me I wasn't supposed to be hitting other children. I tried to explain that I wasn't hitting but playing. I spent the rest of the day in her office until school was over. When I went home, I told my mother. The next morning there was a confrontation and the principal apologized after Mom talked to her. I remember that there was a boy in sixth grade when I was in first grade. I was scared to go to school because he was always picking on me. Mom told them it was the last time she was coming to school because someone was picking on me. I have friends that I met in grade school that are still my best friends today.

What do you remember of the marches?

Ollie Marshal: I remember one of the first marches from Green Memorial Church to town hall. There were a bunch of ministers from Massachusetts. People were jeering from the sides. At first we didn't get protection. We didn't have anyone on our side. The police were there, but they weren't protecting us. When we got to town hall, we got on our knees and prayed.

Ruth: Mom heard a thump and our older brother Bill cry out after the sheriff deputy hit him. She told the deputy that she would take the next lick. She said the football team was around her like backup and the deputy backed off. The deputy told her if she went to heaven then he wanted to go to hell. Mom said, "In hell you'll lift up your eyes to see me." She had no fear. If she died doing this, then this is what God had intended for her life. She was not going to allow anyone to treat her or anyone's children with disrespect. Sarah Small was pregnant with her last child, Freeda, at that time when the same deputy dragged her into jail.

Ollie: Sarah Small sat in the street and they [the police] dragged her to town hall. We went to St. Augustine, Florida, as a group and marched there, too. Dogs were turned on us there in St. Augustine. We moved to Massachusetts soon after that. We didn't march in Massachusetts, but we did a lot of concerts in Massachusetts to raise money. We went from Massachusetts to Maine and did concerts there, too. People would sing freedom songs arranged by Sarah Small.

What was your mother, Mary Mobley, like?

Ruth: I knew if someone had done something to me, all I had to do was get to my mother. Everyone's fight was her fight. She didn't have any fear. She would rather die than let anyone mistreat her or any of her children. We were coming back on a bus from Massachusetts, and a man was bothering a little girl. Mother put the girl in the seat in front of her beside our sister. When the man reached for the girl, she hit his hand away with her fist. Mom said if he touched her again, she would break it. Everyone started cheering, saying they were glad she finally shut him up.

Where did her fight come from?

Ruth: Her mother; she was a strong person.

Ollie: My mother started cleaning houses and wouldn't let people talk down to her. She said if the movement came to Williamston she was going to be a part of it. Protestors came to the building and they locked the doors. She was the cook at Shamrock. She threw off her apron and unlocked the door so that the protestors could get in. She was finished with Shamrock. That is when she became a part of the movement.

Did she ever get paid by the SCLC or other organizations?

Ruth: No, she was never paid. Everything she did was from her heart. Father was supportive of her. He was a logger who worked for the same [white] man for 50 years. Father never tried to stop her from going to the marches. Her children were always taken care of. She never left her children unattended. I was always watched by my grandmother or godparents. Father had a pickup truck from his job. He was told not to use the truck to haul "those" people. He didn't listen because he used the truck to transport protestors. He supported mother and civil rights 100 percent.

Civil rights for her was never about hatred, but about doing what is right. She hated the way people were treated; it was about equality of people. People deserved to be treated equally. Religion played a critical role. Women were going out with only a few men; they had to have faith. Sarah Small was a prayer warrior, Mom was a straight up warrior, and Frinks was just golden. If fighting had to be done, my mother was ready. She didn't have any fear. She had seen so much prejudice, and she was tired of it.

Ollie: I did a lot of marching, singing, and going to jail, but the Massachusetts preachers brought attention. At the jail in St. Augustine, we were served baby food. All the women were packed in one cell. We had to go to the bathroom in front of everyone. I said I wouldn't go to jail for anybody.

Ruth: Mom was proud that she raised six kids and that they never went to jail except in civil rights work. I grew up with an attitude that I could be anything I wanted to be. I was at the top of my class in school.

Ollie: Education was very important; Mom made sure we went to school.

What was Golden Frinks like?

Ruth: I knew him as a little girl; he stayed in court a lot because of the movement. I think a lot of things got turned around and anything they could put on him they did. He was a known agitator, and I think a lot of things he got accused of he wasn't guilty of doing. He would give people the shirt off his back as well as the shirt off anyone who was with him. He was a good man. He loved his family. He had to have a wife who was a godsend. He was gone most of the time. He was a good man, and he believed in what he was doing. He was someone who could get things done.

Ollie: Golden was really the person who got it started. He always knew if you wanted to get something done, you focused on young kids. At E.J. Hayes we protested over the fact that we always got the used stuff.

Joseph Thigpen

White County Commissioner
Interview by Amanda Hilliard Smith
April 12, 2008

What was it like being a county commissioner during desegregation?

I was a county commissioner and responsible for the courthouse in the 1960s. I was aware of what was going on with the law enforcement at that time. We had an integrated police and sheriff's force before the movement even started. Only one person got hurt, and I was the one who took him to Dr. L.C. Wynne. The doctor was a black man who told him he shouldn't have been involved. The man who was hit attempted to hit a black officer and white officers responded.

Williamston was selected because Golden Frinks lived nearby in Edenton. Frinks was too well known in Edenton for being a scoundrel to hold the protest there. They picked Williamston because it was close enough so that they could meet with the folks. Ahoskie's blacks were well off and would not allow outsiders to stir up trouble. In Williamston they found some local women who were interested in their cause.

People on both sides were restrained. The only time there were arrests was when they provoked the town council into arresting them. They would refuse to get a parade permit. The only time there were arrests was when it was scheduled to happen. When blacks threw soda bottles at the police, there was a show of strength, but they were not aggressive about it.

The night they announced they would make no attempt to follow the law, then we had about 75 to 80 arrests. The kids who were arrested were given $25 each. When we arrested them the kids would tell us that they had enough money to get out in the morning, but they wanted to spend the night. Roy Peele was the jailer and he told them that he would make it as comfortable as he could. It was summertime and the jail was located in a residential area. They started singing freedom songs and around 11 p.m. Peele told them to simmer down. He told them he would have to close the windows if they didn't stop. In the morning many of them decided they didn't want to do it again. Bail cost about $15 so they only made a net profit of about $10.

What was Golden Frinks like?

Frinks wasn't a bad person to talk to, but he was a plumber. He could make more money with less work with the SCLC than plumbing. He was a little belligerent but I didn't take too much offense. During a county commissioner meeting, he barged in to tell us a few things. I physically escorted him out because he wasn't going to interrupt business. I was serious about him not being in the room without an appointment. Later on he was in the hospital in Ahoskie, and I went to see him. So there were no hard feelings between us.

What did you think of the Northern ministers coming to Williamston?

All the stories in the Northern press were totally different from what was going on. Everything that went out of here made the blacks look like they were in bondage. Then these outsiders would come in and move in with black families. They would even have sit-ins in local churches and sleep in the churches. This was really offensive to members. They were Episcopalians, but the local church didn't like it much either. The Episcopalian minister was a young guy named Bill Campbell. He went with me up to Boston to speak to their media. WBZ in Boston was the biggest radio in the Northeast. It was all a set up when they invited us. Everything was loaded against us. It was a call-in show that lasted two to three hours. The fellow who ran the show was pro-integration. I pointed out that all the staff in the studio from the doorman to the engineers were white. He cut off the microphone and told us not to talk about the station. So of course we did mention it one more time. The next day there was an ad in the paper saying WBZ was seeking black employees. No one has ever determined who in Williamston bought the ad. After that, they stopped taking calls about Williamston, and we had no more visitors from up north.

We didn't have any problems despite the reports of how terrible we were. Only thing I know that was reprehensible was one or two boys would make it tough on their automobiles. The outsiders would escort the black girls around town. Then the boys would tie a rod on the back of their pickup truck and ram it into their radiator. Everybody was on the edge and affected by it.

You may have a black maid and all of a sudden you had to be careful around her. You didn't do as much kidding between the races. Everybody was stiff-legged. This created a divide within the black community. Here you had women who were more interested in integration than working.

What do you think kept Williamston from becoming violent?

Blacks did minor things, but they didn't do anything that was violent to speak of and the law enforcement didn't do anything to stir them up. Everyone realized that this was a planned event. Mr. Green, the mayor, was a level-headed businessman that was friends with everybody. There was also a labor relations board with members from both sides of the black community. There were certain groups of blacks that didn't like others stirring up trouble. Frinks' job was to stir up and create problems of other people, despite the fact that the whites and about 75 percent of blacks didn't want the movement. The best blacks were on the side of the status quo. All it would have taken was a few hot heads on either side to come to violence. I think the mayor did a good job tranquilizing the situation.

Every once in a while you would have someone shooting a BB gun into a windshield. There were plenty of people who were willing, but the police were just as interested in preserving the peace. Whites had all the guns and ammunition. Participants were mostly teenagers and smaller. They would meet in Green Memorial, and you could hear them arguing to break the law. It was a pep rally, and it took them several weeks to get enough organization to get a public showing. Everyone was talking about it, but not any real action.

I was vice-chairman at the time. It caused us a little extra work and concern. It wasn't an uprising of the people. We didn't appreciate having to hire extra officers. Mr. Green, the mayor, was popular and deserved a lot of credit. The management was resilient and had many meetings with the black community. He would go over their list of demands and would explain why they weren't fixed. We realized that the instructions were coming from out of town and might not meet the needs in

Williamston as in other places. They made demands like hiring a black sheriff, which wasn't under the mayor's power.

We didn't have any Bull Connors here so we didn't have the violence. It was a situation where we were sitting on a fuse—it had to be primed. It was all a planned event to bring about the Civil Rights Act. Credit should go to the black community, a sensible police chief, and a gentle sheriff. Local folks had to deal with the hard feelings when they left. All boards would have had black representatives if it were up to the county.

Brenda Whelchel

White Student
Interview by Amanda Hilliard Smith
October 7, 2005

What was it like being a student during desegregation?

It was pretty normal. I was the first class that graduated with two blacks. We did not have any blacks in school until my senior year. Before integration we would have bomb threats and people would start rumors that blacks were coming to the school to start trouble. Basically, I was more scared of what the white people would say than what the blacks ever did. The blacks had demonstrations. They would gather at different places to sing "We Shall Overcome" and other songs. I would just stay out of their way.

I lived a couple of miles from the school. To show my lack of fear, I walked home from school every day right through the black community. I never had any problems. We have a railroad trestle near our house. There were periods of time people would get on the trestle and throw things at the school buses. My dad had an agreement with the police department where he would stand guard so that the buses could get through.

The two black students who came in our senior year were very quiet and kept to themselves. They seemed to be very smart kids. I never talked to them. They were not in any of my classes and our paths did not cross. Other students would speak to them but no one went out of their way to be extra-friendly to them. I always felt that they were very sad and lonely to be in a school where they didn't feel welcome. But there was no hostility shown to them. They did participate in some extracurricular activities and were in the upper-level classes. They were welcome to join in. The parents had more of a problem with integration than the students did.

What was the first day of school like?

It was a normal day. I don't recall seeing police in riot gear. It was as normal a year as can be expected for a senior. They were the only two blacks to come into the high school in 1964–65 school year. More black students came in afterward. Before the year started there were demonstrations. The kids were okay with it but the parents wanted to make a big deal out of it. If the adults had left it alone, I think there would have been a smoother transition. The most violence I can recall is a rock being thrown or name calling. The KKK burned a cross and that was very offensive to me. At graduation there were no problems. They walked in like the rest of us. Their parents were welcomed like the rest of the parents. We had around 100 students in the class of '65, which was the biggest class at that time.

What rumors were there at this time?

We had a lot of rumors but they were not founded. We had one rumor that there was a group of blacks that were going to march on the high school. It was in the first semester, but not at the beginning of the year. It was taken seriously enough that they let school out that day. A group of parents came out in their pickup trucks with hoes, shovels, and I don't know what else. I don't know if they had guns but I never saw any. We were dismissed from school and only told that there was a problem. Not knowing what that problem was I walked right into the area that they said they were coming in from. I never saw a soul. When I got back to school the next day they told us what happened. It was just an adult rumor mill because the kids were very tolerant. They handled it better than the adults did.

Do you think gradual integration was preferable to immediate integration?

I think it caused fewer problems than trying to force people into something. Human nature is opposed to change. If you do it gently it is received better.

Willis Williams

Black Activist
Interview by Amanda Hilliard Smith
June 8, 2011

Can you tell me about Joe Cross?

I was 15 years old in 1957. My older brother was four years older and the same age as Joe Cross. They were both sophomore students at A&T. He [Joe] stayed with his stepfather in Williamston. His stepfather was a carpenter. Joe would come to the house to pick up my brother. Joe had a car and my brother would ride with him.

I was one of eight children. I had two sisters and one brother in college. They had planned to go back late Saturday evening—around dusk, 8 p.m. We had a dog but when company came, it was my dog. I had to keep the dog in check so that the dog wouldn't bother them. I was outside waiting for Joe to pick my brother up. There was no pavement at the time so I saw dust coming. I could see Joe's car with two sheriff deputies following behind. I noticed that they were going faster then normal. They pulled into the yard. The deputies put Joe in one of the deputy's car and another deputy drove Joe's car. I relayed what I saw to my brother and father, but we didn't have a phone. We were trying to figure out how my brother would get back to school.

Watson Waters worked for the county using the road dragger. Early Sunday morning, we heard the equipment smoothing up the road. It took him a couple of hours to smooth the three-mile circle. The tracks were gone with any evidence.

My father went to Jesse Rogers [Joe's stepfather] and found out Joe had been killed. They convened a grand jury; the police asked Father if he wanted me to stay in the jail for protection. My father didn't agree with that. I was going to be one of the key witnesses to the whole thing. The defense tried to say I was just a child and it was a figment of my imagination. I knew what I saw; it was not something you make up. The jury acquitted the deputy.

Sheriff Rawls had different versions. What I saw and heard didn't change. We were fortunate that Joe didn't pick my brother up before he was caught. The story was that he was seeing a waitress at Breezewood called Polly Roberson. Joe was working in the shipyard that summer in Norfolk, Virginia. The sheriff's department said he had been coming from Norfolk to stalk Polly Roberson. They said she had called the sheriff's office because she was afraid for her life. They were trying to catch him in the act. They said he tried to escape from Williamston. The sheriff's department said he didn't come as far as our house.

How did the black community feel about this case?

They knew what the atmosphere was like in Martin County. There had lots of incidents with the Klan. Blacks were not allowed to date white females. The KKK was here in the 1950s. The black community said that he was murdered because the lady said he was making advances. The white community said the opposite; it was because he was harassing. The NAACP tried to mount a protest.

Lots of stuff going on—racial tensions—at that time, a white farmer had killed a black tenant farmer. The town hired a black cop as a way to try to fix the situation. It is connected—the all-white judge, jury, and sheriff's department. No black people in the government role.

The blacks started looking at voting rights as an avenue to influence decisions. My mom and father had to read the Constitution to register to vote. The schools were segregated. We were trying to get equal access to education. Martin County was controlled by the farming industry. You don't need education to work on a farm. There were not even a lot of white kids getting a higher education.

The SCLC and Golden Frinks were working in eastern North Carolina. One community started to be successful, and it spread through the churches. The blacks find out that they have the power to stand up. Churches were prevalent because they provided meeting places; we couldn't use the schools or public facilities.

What was Golden Frinks like?

I knew Golden Frinks really well. Golden was in the middle of all of it. We did a lot of communication and planning. Frinks was easy to work with. He knew how to organize. He knew what pressures to bring to get attention. The national SCLC trained him well in how to do that. He was liked and loved by a lot people, black people. He was a good guy. Frinks had a plan. Some people didn't like his methods. Since it was a black church movement, some people believed in waiting for God. Frinks believed that you had to take a firm stance. He was accused of doing it for the money, but he did it from the heart as far as I know. He had to be kind of secretive because people wanted to see him gone.

Chapter Notes

Preface

1. Willis Williams, interview by author, July 7, 2005.

2. Adam Fairclough, *To Redeem the Soul of America: The Southern Christian Leadership Conference and Martin Luther King, Jr.* (Athens: University of Georgia Press, 1987), 3–4.

3. Haul Reddick, interview by author, Mar. 27, 2008.

4. "Judicial Order May Avert Threatened Race Violence," *The Robesonian*, Nov. 14, 1963.

5. "'Bill of Rights?' But This Is Williamston and We Have Rules Here, Police Said," *Vineyard Gazette*, May 8, 1964.

6. See Ruth Spruill, interview by author, June 9, 2011; Simon Wendt, "They Finally Found Out That We Really Are Men: Violence, Non-Violence, and Black Manhood in the Civil Rights Era," *Gender & History* 19 (Nov. 2007): 544.

7. Charles Bullock and Harrell Rogers, "Coercion to Compliance: Southern School Districts and School Desegregation Guidelines," *The Journal of Politics* 38 (Nov. 1976): 1004.

8. David Garrow, *Bearing the Cross: Martin Luther King, Jr., and the Southern Christian Leadership Conference* (New York: Perennial Classics, 1999), 291.

Chapter One

1. Willis Williams, interview by author, June 8, 2011.

2. See Francis Manning, "Joseph J. Cross Fatally Wounded Saturday Night," *The Enterprise*, Sept. 10, 1957; Francis Mitchell, "Did NC Whites Kill A&T Student by Mistake?" *Jet*, Nov. 14, 1957; W.H. Scarborough, "The Strange Case of Joe Cross," *The Chapel Hill Weekly*, Aug. 19, 1964; David Lilienthal, Jr., "Two Williamston Murders were Investigated by the Chapel Hill and Vineyard Reporters," *Vineyard Gazette*, Aug. 7, 1964; David Carter, "The Williamston Freedom Movement: Civil Rights at the Grass Roots in Eastern North Carolina, 1957–1964," *The North Carolina Historical Review* 157 (Jan. 1999): 3–5.

3. See David Lilienthal, Jr., "Two Williamston Murders were Investigated by the Chapel Hill and Vineyard Reporters," *Vineyard Gazette*, Aug. 7, 1964; David Carter, "The Williamston Freedom Movement: Civil Rights at the Grass Roots in Eastern North Carolina, 1957–1964," *The North Carolina Historical Review* 157 (Jan. 1999): 3–5.

4. See Francis Mitchell, "Did NC Whites Kill A&T Student by Mistake?" *Jet*, Nov. 14, 1957; W.H. Scarborough, "The Strange Case of Joe Cross," *The Chapel Hill Weekly*, Aug. 19, 1964; William Earl Newsome, interview by author, Dec. 28, 2012.

5. Francis Mitchell, "Did NC Whites Kill A&T Student by Mistake?" *Jet*, Nov. 14, 1957.

6. See Willis Williams, interview by author, June 8, 2011; W.H. Scarborough, "The Strange Case of Joe Cross," *The Chapel Hill Weekly*, Aug. 19, 1964; David Lilienthal, Jr., "Two Williamston Murders Were Investigated by the Chapel Hill and Vineyard Reporters," *Vineyard Gazette*, Aug. 7, 1964; Francis Manning, "Thirty-Six Criminals Cases Set for Trial," *The Enterprise*, Sept. 19, 1957.

7. U.S. Bureau of the Census, *Characteristics of the Population*, 1960 (Washington, DC: Government Printing Office, 1965).

8. Charles Bullock and Harrell Rogers, "Coercion to Compliance: Southern School Districts and School Desegregation Guidelines," *The Journal of Politics* 38 (Nov. 1976): 1004.

9. See David Cecelski, *Along Freedom Road: Hyde County, North Carolina, and the Fate of Black Schools in the South* (Chapel Hill: University of North Carolina Press, 1994), 177; W.H. Scarborough, "Williamston: Future Is Anything But Rosy," *The Chapel Hill Weekly*, Aug. 30, 1964; U.S. Bureau of the Census, *Characteristics of the Population*, 1960 (Washington, DC: Government Printing Office, 1965); Beth Vanfossen, "Variables Related to Resistance to Desegregation in the South," *Social Forces* 47, no. 1 (Sept. 1968): 44.

10. See Pete Daniels, *The Lost Social Revolution: The South in the 1950s* (Chapel Hill: University of North Carolina Press, 2000), 214; David Lilienthal, Jr., "Williamston's Economic Future Is Bound to the Presence, or Absence, of Racial Tensions," *Vineyard Gazette*, Aug. 11, 1964; W.H. Scarborough, "Williamston: Future Is Anything But Rosy," *The Chapel Hill Weekly*, Aug. 30, 1964.

11. See W.H. Scarborough, "Williamston and the Law," *The Chapel Hill Weekly*, Aug. 23, 1964; Francis Manning, "Man Critically Wounded and Women Killed in the County," *The Enterprise*, Aug. 13, 1957; Francis Manning, "Thirty-Six Criminal Cases Set for Trial," *The Enterprise*, Sept. 19, 1957; David Carter, "The Williamston Freedom Movement: Civil Rights at the Grass Roots in Eastern North Carolina," *The North Carolina Historical Review* 157 (Jan. 1999): 1–3; Francis Manning, "L.C. Moore Freed in Biggs Murder Case," *The Enterprise*, Oct. 1, 1957.

12. See W.H. Scarborough, "Williamston and the Law," *The Chapel Hill Weekly*, Aug. 23, 1964; W.H. Scarborough, "The Charge of Brutality," *The Chapel Hill Weekly*, Aug. 9, 1964; Willis Williams interview by author, June 8, 2011.

Chapter Two

1. See David Carter, "The Williamston Freedom Movement: Civil Rights at the Grass Roots in Eastern North Carolina," *The North Carolina Historical Review* 157 (Jan. 1999): 9; Francis Mitchell, "Did NC Whites Kill A&T Student by Mistake?" *Jet*, Nov. 14, 1957.

2. See David Lilienthal, "Golden Frinks, Hated by Whites, Exercises a Unique Influence in a Divided Williamston," *Vineyard Gazette*, July 28, 1964; David Carter, "The Williamston Freedom Movement: Civil Rights at the Grass Roots in Eastern North Carolina," *The North Carolina Historical Review* 157 (Jan. 1999): 9; Francis Manning, *The Enterprise*, Apr. 13, 1963; Francis Manning, "Record Vote Cast Yesterday in the Primary Election," *The Enterprise*, Apr. 16, 1963.

3. See David Garrow, *Bearing the Cross: Martin Luther King, Jr., and the Southern Christian Leadership Conference* (New York: Perennial Classics, 1999), 163; Golden Frinks, "Report on North Carolina," Southern Christian Leadership Conference papers, Apr. 10, 1963; W.H. Scarborough, "Golden Frinks: The Sparkplug," *The Chapel Hill Weekly*, Aug. 2, 1964; David Lilienthal, Jr., "Golden Frinks, Hated by Whites, Exercises a Unique Influence in a Divided Williamston," *Vineyard Gazette*, July 28, 1964; David Carter, "The Williamston Freedom Movement: Civil Rights at the Grass Roots in Eastern North Carolina," *The North Carolina Historical Review* 157 (Jan. 1999): 10.

4. Goldie Frinks Wells and Crystal Sanders, *Golden Asro Frinks Telling the Unsung Song* (Salt Lake City: Aardvark Global, 2009), 70.

5. See Ida Speller, reflection, July 30, 2011; "SCLC States First Protest Demonstration in Williamston, NC," Southern Christian Leadership Conference Press Release, July 1, 1963.

6. See Ida Speller, reflection, July 30, 2011; W.H. Scarborough, "Segregated-est Town in the U.S.A.," *The Chapel Hill Weekly*, July 26, 1964; Alma Purvis, interview by author, July 29, 2011.

7. See Alma Purvis, interview by author, July 29, 2011; Francis King, interview by author, Oct. 22, 2005; Simon Wendt, "They Finally Found Out That We Really Are Men: Violence, Non-Violence, and Black Manhood in the Civil Rights Era," *Gender & History* 19 (Nov. 2007): 544; Bob Purvis, interview by author, July 29, 2011; Ida Speller, reflection, July 30, 2011.

8. See Booker Small and Ida Small Speller, *Sarah Small's Freedom Fighters Legacy*, directed by Booker Small (Boston: Longshots Videographer, 2011), film; Styron Bond, Jr., interview by author, Mar. 1, 2008.

9. See Bob Purvis, interview, July 29, 2011; Alma Purvis, interview, July 29, 2011; Francis King, interview, Oct. 22, 2005; David Carter, "The Williamston Freedom Movement: Civil Rights at the Grass Roots in Eastern North Carolina," *The North Carolina Historical Review* 157 (Jan. 1999): 17.

10. Allen Critcher III, "Local Civil Rights Leader Recalls the Movement," *The Enterprise Centennial Edition* (Sept. 1999): 31.

11. David Lilienthal, Jr., "Golden Frinks, Hated by Whites, Exercises a Unique Influence in a Divided Williamston," *Vineyard Gazette*, July 28, 1964.

12. Ida Speller, interview by author, July 13, 2011.

Chapter Three

1. See W.H. Scarborough, "Golden Frinks: The Sparkplug," *The Chapel Hill Weekly*, Aug. 2, 1964; David Cecelski, *Along Freedom Road: Hyde County, North Carolina, and the Fate of Black Schools in the South* (Chapel Hill: University of North Carolina Press, 1994), 83–84.

2. See Alma Purvis, interview by author, July 29, 2011; Ruth Spruill, interview by author, July 9, 2011; "SCLC States First Protest Demonstration in Williamston, NC," Southern Christian Leadership Conference Press Release, July 1, 1963; Ida Speller, reflection, July 30, 2011; W.H. Scarborough, "Golden Frinks: The Sparkplug," *The Chapel Hill Weekly*, Aug. 2, 1964.

3. See Ida Speller, reflection, July 30, 2011; David Lilienthal, Jr., "Golden Frinks, Hated by Whites, Exercises a Unique Influence in a Divided Williamston," *Vineyard Gazette*, July 28, 1964; David Carter, "The Williamston Freedom Movement: Civil Rights at the Grass Roots in Eastern North Carolina," *The North Carolina Historical Review* 157 (Jan. 1999): 16; Styron Bond, Jr., interview by author, Mar. 1, 2008; Jonathan Clayborne, "Change Has Come to Williamston," *Washington Daily News*, Feb. 7, 2005.

4. See Daniel Harrell, Jr., "Report to Reverend Andrew Young," Southern Christian Leadership Conference Papers, Jan. 24, 1964; Ida Speller, reflection, July 30, 2011; Alma Purvis, interview by author, July 29, 2011.

5. See Allen Critcher III, "Local Civil Rights Leader Recalls the Movement," *The Enterprise Centennial Edition* (Sept. 1999): 32; Ruth Spruill, interview by author, July 9, 2011.

6. "Negro's Claim Is Disputed," *The News and Observer*, July 10, 1963.

7. See David Lilienthal, Jr., "Golden Frinks, Hated by Whites, Exercises a Unique Influence in a Divided Williamston," *Vineyard Gazette*, July 28, 1964; W. H. Scarborough, "The Charges of Brutality," *The Chapel Hill Weekly*, Aug. 9, 1964.

8. Ida Speller, reflection, July 30, 2011.

9. See Golden Frinks, "Report from North Carolina," Southern Christian Leadership Conference Papers, Aug. 9, 1963; David E. Lilienthal, "Agitators and Outsiders Are Not Welcome by the White People in Racially Tense Williamston," *Vineyard Gazette*, July 31, 1964.

10. See Marie Robertson, interview by author, Oct. 7, 2005; Alton Hopewell, interview by author, June 22, 2005.

11. See W.H. Scarborough, "Segregatedest Town in the U.S.A.," *The Chapel Hill Weekly*, July 26, 1964; Joseph Thigpen, interview by author, Apr. 12, 2008.

12. See W.H. Scarborough, "Golden Frinks: The Sparkplug," *The Chapel Hill Weekly*, Aug. 2, 1964.

13. See Bob Purvis, interview, July 29,

2011; James Small, "Williamston Speaks: The Voice of Williamston, NC," Southern Christian Leadership Conference Papers; Ida Speller, reflection, July 30, 2011.

14. Willis Williams, interview by author, June 8, 2011.

Chapter Four

1. W.H. Scarborough, "The Charges of Brutality," *The Chapel Hill Weekly*, Aug. 9, 1964.

2. See David Lilienthal, Jr., "Williamston Klansman Talks Without Restraint About His Position in Town's Racial Struggle," *Vineyard Gazette*, Aug. 14, 1964; W.H. Scarborough, "The Klan Raises Its Cross Again," *The Chapel Hill Weekly*, July 29, 1964; W.H. Scarborough, "Segregated-est Town in the U.S.A.," *The Chapel Hill Weekly*, July 26, 1964.

3. See David Lilienthal, Jr., "Golden Frinks, Hated by Whites, Exercises a Unique Influence in a Divided Williamston, *Vineyard Gazette*, July 28, 1964; Allen Critcher III, "Local Civil Rights Leader Recalls the Movement," *The Enterprise Centennial Edition* (Sept. 1999): 32; Ida Speller, reflection, July 30, 2011; W.H. Scarborough, "The Charges of Brutality," *The Chapel Hill Weekly*, Aug. 9, 1964.

4. See Ida Speller, reflection, July 30, 2011; "Demonstrations in Williamston Are Suspended," *Daily Reflector*, Aug. 2, 1963; W.H. Scarborough, "The Charges of Brutality," *The Chapel Hill Weekly*, Aug. 9, 1964; "North Carolina and the Negro," *NC Mayor's Co-operating Committee*, 1964; David Carter, "The Williamston Freedom Movement: Civil Rights at the Grass Roots in Eastern North Carolina," *The North Carolina Historical Review* 157 (Jan. 1999): 22; Betsy Conway, interview by author, July 17, 2011.

5. See "Sanford Asks Mayors for Racial Crisis Aid," *The News and Observer*, July 6, 1963; W.H. Scarborough, "Segregated-est Town in the U.S.A.," *The Chapel Hill Weekly*, July 26, 1964; W.H. Scarborough, "Williamston and the Silence of the Whites," *The Chapel Hill Weekly*, Aug. 26, 1964; David Lilienthal, Jr., "Agitators and Outsiders Are Not Welcome by the White People in Racially Tense Williamston," *Vineyard Gazette,* July 31, 1964.

6. Chelsea R. Watson, "A Historical Analysis of the Civil Rights Movement in Windsor, Bertie County, North Carolina, 1963–1968" (masters dissertation, Morgan State University, Dec. 2007), 40.

7. See Ed Clayton, "SCLC Gains Major Break-Through in Williamston, NC," Southern Christian Leadership Conference Papers, Jan. 4, 1964; W.H. Scarborough, "The Charge of Brutality," *The Chapel Hill Weekly,* Aug. 9, 1964.

8. See "Williamston Mayor Denies Council Held Secret Meeting," *News and Observer*, Aug. 10, 1964. "North Carolina and the Negro," *NC Mayor's Co-operating Committee*, 1964; Golden Frinks, "Report from North Carolina," Southern Christian Leadership Conference Papers, Aug. 9, 1963.

9. See "Williamston Mayor Denies Council Held Secret Meeting," *News and Observer,* Aug. 10, 1963; George Corey, interview by author, July 17, 2011.

10. Ida Speller, reflection, July 30, 2011.

11. See Francis King, interview by author, Oct. 22, 2005; "Martin Negroes Going to Court," *News and Observer*, Aug. 11, 1963; Alma Purvis, interview by author, July 29, 2011; Ida Speller, interview by author, July 13, 2011; "Judge Requests Briefs Be Filed," *News and Observer*, Aug. 18, 1963.

12. See Martin County Court Record, Justice of Peace Court, Aug. 10, 1963; Styron Bond, Jr., interview by author, Mar. 1, 2008.

13. See Francis Manning, "County Jailer Ends Thirty-Year Term," *The Enterprise*, June 30, 1963; Golden Frinks, "Report on North Carolina," Southern Christian Leadership Conference Papers, Aug. 9, 1963; Ida Speller, reflection, July 30, 2011.

14. See Joseph Thigpen, interview by author, Apr. 12, 2008; Ralph Hargett, interview by author, Oct. 29, 2012; Ida Speller, reflection, July 30, 2011.

15. See Alma Purvis, interview by author, July 29, 2011; W.H. Scarborough, "The Charge of Brutality," *The Chapel Hill*

Weekly, Aug. 9, 1964; Southern Christian Leadership Conference Press Release, Southern Christian Leadership Conference Papers, Oct. 17, 1963; Clarence Biggs, interview by author, Oct. 6, 2005.

16. See Bob Purvis, interview by author, July 29, 2011; Ruth Spruill, interview by author, July 9, 2011; Ida Speller, interview by author, July 13, 2011.

17. See W.H. Scarborough, "The Charges of Brutality," *The Chapel Hill Weekly,* Aug. 9, 1964; Joseph Thigpen, interview by author, Apr. 12, 2008.

Chapter Five

1. See Styron Bond, Jr., interview by author, Mar. 1, 2008; Jackie Bond, interview by author, Jan. 18, 2012; Daniel Harrell, Jr., "Report to SCLC," Southern Christian Leadership Conference Papers.

2. See Nelson Harris, "The Implementation of the Desegregation Decision in North Carolina," *The Journal of Negro History* 34, no. 3 (Summer 1955): 310–317; Martin County Board of Education, Minutes, Book 5, 1959–1976, Williamston, NC, 76.

3. See Ralph Hargett, interview by author, Oct. 29, 2012; Styron Bond, Jr., interview by author, Mar. 1, 2008; Alma Purvis, interview by author, July 29, 2011.

4. See W.H. Scarborough, "Williamston and the Law," *The Chapel Hill Weekly,* Aug. 23, 1964; Goldie Frinks Wells and Crystal Sanders, *Golden Asro Frinks Telling the Unsung Song* (Salt Lake City: Aardvark Global, 2009), 83.

5. See W.H. Scarborough, "Williamston and the Law," *The Chapel Hill Weekly,* Aug. 23, 1964; Clarence Biggs, interview by author, Oct. 6, 2005; Jackie Bond, interview by author, Jan. 18, 2012.

6. See Ida Speller, reflection, July 30, 2011; Styron Bond, Jr., interview by author, Mar. 1, 2008; Jonathan Clayborne, "Martin County's Bloody Sunday," *Washington Daily News,* Feb. 13, 2005; David Carter, "The Williamston Freedom Movement: Civil Rights at the Grass Roots in Eastern North Carolina, 1957–1964," *The North Carolina Historical Review* 157 (Jan. 1999): 26.

7. See Charles Bond, "Negro Family Not Hurt, Shots Fired into Store," *Virginian-Pilot,* Sept. 20, 1963; Phyllis Ryan, "Acts of Violence in Williamston," Southern Christian Leadership Conference Papers, Apr. 20, 1964; W.H. Scarborough, "Williamston and the Law," *The Chapel Hill Weekly,* Aug. 23, 1964.

8. See "156 NC Teachers Protest Police Methods," *Journal and Guide,* Sept. 21, 1963; Ed Clayton, "Williamston, NC, Voice Protest Against Police Brutality," Southern Christian Leadership Conference Papers, Sept. 9, 1963; Clarence Biggs, interview by author, Oct. 6, 2005; Richard Eugene Rogers, interview by author, Oct. 9, 2005.

9. Francis King, interview by author, Oct. 22, 2005.

10. See Francis Manning, *The Enterprise,* Sept. 4, 1964; Martin County Board of Education, Minutes, Book 5, 1959–1976, Williamston, NC, Sept. 3, 1964.

11. See Bob Purvis, interview by author, July 29, 2011; Francis King, interview by author, Oct. 22, 2005; Styron Bond, Jr., interview by author, Mar. 1, 2008.

12. See Martin County Board of Education, Minutes, Book 5, 1959–1976, Williamston, NC, 77; Richard Eugene Rogers, interview by author, Oct. 9, 2005.

13. Clarence Biggs, interview by author, Oct. 6, 2005.

14. See Francis Manning, "Attendance Gains In County Schools," *The Enterprise,* Sept. 10, 1963; Richard Eugene Rogers, interview by author, Oct. 9, 2005.

15. Alma Purvis, interview, July 29, 2011.

Chapter Six

1. "Judicial Order May Avert Threatened Race Violence," *The Robesonian,* Nov. 14, 1963.

2. See Reverend Paul Chapman, Autobiography (2000); David Garrow, *Bearing the Cross: Martin Luther King, Jr., and the Southern Christian Leadership Conference* (New York: Perennial Classics, 1999), 291.

3. Reverend Paul Chapman, Autobiography (2000); Reverend Paul Chapman, interview by Linsey Lee, Martha's Vineyard Museum Oral History Center, Sept. 26, 2008.

4. See David Lilienthal, Jr., "Goes to North Carolina in Cause of Civil Rights," *Vineyard Gazette*, Nov. 15, 1963; Styron Bond, Jr., interview by author, Mar. 1, 2008.

5. W.H. Scarborough, "Williamston and the Silence of the Whites," *The Chapel Hill Weekly*, Aug. 26, 1964.

6. See "Goes to North Carolina in Cause of Civil Rights," *Vineyard Gazette*, Nov. 15, 1963; Reverend Paul Chapman, interview by Linsey Lee, Martha's Vineyard Museum Oral History Center, Sept. 26, 2008; Reverend Henry Byrd, interview by Linsey Lee, Martha's Vineyard Museum Oral History Center, Nov. 25, 1993.

7. See "Judicial Order May Avert Threatened Race Violence," *The Robesonian*, Nov. 14, 1963; "Williamston Race Crisis Back Again," *News and Observer*, Nov. 14, 1963; Francis Manning, "Temporary Injunction Issued Against Illegal Marching Here," *The Enterprise*, Nov. 14, 1963; Reverend Paul Chapman, Autobiography (2000).

8. See "Rev. Henry Byrd Released from Jail in Williamston," *Vineyard Gazette*, Nov. 22, 1963; "15 Ministers, 78 Negroes Arrested at Williamston," *News and Observer*, Nov. 15, 1964; "Demonstrators in Appearance Here," *Daily Reflector*, Nov. 18, 1963; Styron Bond, Jr., interview by author, Mar. 1, 2008; Reverend Paul Chapman, interview by Linsey Lee, Martha's Vineyard Museum Oral History Center, Sept. 26, 2008.

9. See Reverend Paul Chapman, Autobiography (2000); Reverend Paul Chapman, interview by Linsey Lee, Martha's Vineyard Museum Oral History Center, Sept. 26, 2008.

10. See "Williamston," *Charlotte News*, Nov. 18, 1963; Goldie Frinks Wells and Crystal Sanders, *Golden Asro Frinks: Telling the Unsung Song* (Salt Lake City: Aardvark Global, 2009), 83; Ashley Futrell, "Editorial," *The Washington Daily News*, Nov. 20, 1963.

11. Howard Groover, "The Crisis of Our Times," *The Enterprise*, Nov. 21, 1963.

12. Francis Manning, "Press Reports Taken to Task by WNCT, Greenville," *The Enterprise*, Nov. 19, 1963.

13. Ida Speller, interview by author, July 13, 2011.

14. David Garrow, *Bearing the Cross: Martin Luther King, Jr., and the Southern Christian Leadership Conference* (New York: Perennial Classics, 1999), 306–7.

15. See Reverend Paul Chapman, Autobiography (2000); David Carter, "The Williamston Freedom Movement: Civil Rights at the Grass Roots in Eastern North Carolina, 1957–1964," *The North Carolina Historical Review* 157 (Jan. 1999): 35; W.H. Scarborough, "Williamston and the Silence of the Whites," *The Chapel Hill Weekly*, Aug. 26, 1964.

16. "Civil Rights Rally by Small Group Yesterday," *The Daily Reflector*, Dec. 16, 1963.

17. See Bob Purvis, interview by author, July 29, 2011; "Don's Buy," flyer, The Williamston Unit of the Southern Christian Leadership Conference; Clarence Biggs, interview by author, Oct. 6, 2005.

18. See David Lilienthal, Jr., "Williamston's Economic Future is Bound to the Presence, or Absence, of Racial Tensions," *Vineyard Gazette*, Aug. 11, 1964; W.H. Scarborough, "Segregated-est Town in the U.S.A.," *The Chapel Hill Weekly*, July 26, 1964.

19. Ollie Marshall, interview by author, July 9, 2011.

20. Ralph Hargett, interview by author, Oct. 29, 2012.

21. See "Freedom Rally Is Marked by Show of Warm Enthusiasm," *Vineyard Gazette*, Jan. 3, 1964; Sunday Smith, "We'll Remember You, New Verse Added to Song," *Vineyard Gazette*, Jan. 3, 1964; Bessie Lee Norton, letter to the editor, *Vineyard Gazette*, Jan. 1, 1964; Bessie Lee Norton, letter to the editor, *Vineyard Gazette*, Jan. 10, 1964; Henry L. Bird, letter to the editor, *Vineyard Gazette*, Jan. 17, 1964.

22. Alma Purvis, interview by author, July 29, 2011.

23. See Reverend Paul Chapman, Autobiography; Reverend Paul Chapman to author, Jan. 26, 2012.

Chapter Seven

1. See W.H. Scarborough, "Williamston and the Silence of the Whites," *The Chapel Hill Weekly,* Aug. 26, 1964; Reverend Paul Chapman to author, Jan. 18, 2012.

2. David Carter, "The Williamston Freedom Movement: Civil Rights at the Grass Roots in Eastern North Carolina, 1957–1964," *The North Carolina Historical Review* 157 (Jan. 1999): 35.

3. Phyllis Ryan, "Massachusetts Unit of Southern Christian Leadership Conference Press Release," Southern Christian Leadership Conference Papers, Mar. 25, 1964.

4. See Joseph Thigpen, interview by author, Apr. 12, 2008; Phyllis Ryan, "Massachusetts Unit of Southern Christian Leadership Conference Press Release," *Southern Christian Leadership Conference Papers,* Mar. 30, 1964; Reverend Paul Chapman, Autobiography (2000).

5. See "Non-Violent Response Can Convert the Violence," *Vineyard Gazette,* Apr. 17, 1964; Phyllis Ryan, "Massachusetts Unit of Southern Christian Leadership Conference Press Release," Southern Christian Leadership Conference Papers, Mar. 30, 1964.

6. Reverend Paul Chapman, interview by Linsey Lee, Martha's Vineyard Museum Oral History Center, Sept. 26, 2008.

7. See W.H. Scarborough, "Williamston and the Silence of the Whites," *The Chapel Hill Weekly,* Aug. 26, 1964; Goldie Frinks Wells and Crystal Sanders, *Golden Asro Frinks: Telling the Unsung Song* (Salt Lake City: Aardvark Global, 2009), 93; "Work Started on Rebuilding of the Church of Advent," *The Enterprise,* Nov. 21, 1963.

8. "Saintly Babes in Tobaccoland," *Herford County Herald,* Nov. 19, 1963.

9. See Phyllis Ryan, "Massachusetts Unit of Southern Christian Leadership Conference Press Release," Southern Christian Leadership Conference Papers, Mar. 30, 1964; Reverend Paul Chapman, Autobiography (2000); Phyllis Ryan, "Acts of Violence in Williamston," Southern Christian Leadership Conference Papers, Apr. 20, 1964; "Williamston Negroes Now in Dire Financial Need," *Vineyard Gazette,* Apr. 3, 1964.

10. See Haul Reddick, interview by author, Mar. 27, 2008; Joseph Thigpen, interview by author, Apr. 12, 2008.

11. See David Lilienthal, Jr., "Two Williamstons," *Vineyard Gazette,* July 24, 1964; George Lawson to David King, "Report from Williamston," June 1, 1964, David King Papers, Duke University Library.

12. David Lilienthal, Jr., "Golden Frinks, Hated by Whites, Exercises a Unique Influence in a Divided Williamston," *Vineyard Gazette,* July 28, 1964.

13. Ida Speller, interview by author, July 13, 2011.

14. See Ralph Hargett, interview by author, Oct. 29, 2012; "New Trial Is Likely for Ralph Hargett," *Vineyard Gazette,* Oct. 2, 1964.

Chapter Eight

1. See David Lilienthal Jr., "Two Williamsons, Tragically Apart, Appear in Joint Investigation Made in Weekly Newspapers," *Vineyard Gazette,* July 24, 1964; "Golden Frinks Brings Message of Non-Violence," *Vineyard Gazette,* May 15, 1964; W.H. Scarborough, "Segregated-est Town in the U.S.A." *The Chapel Hill Weekly,* July 26, 1964; W.H. Scarborough, "The View from Martha's Vineyard," *The Chapel Hill Weekly,* June 10, 1964; W.H. Scarborough, "The Vineyard Ladies Are Right but the Picture Has More to It." *The Chapel Hill Weekly,* June 10, 1964.

2. Editorial, "The Williamston Story: If Nothing Else, an Object Lesson for Us All," *The Chapel Hill Weekly,* August 30, 1964.

3. See "We'll Remember You," *Vineyard Gazette,* January, 3, 1964; Nancy Whiting, interview by Linsey Lee, Martha's Vineyard Museum Oral History Center, Nov. 15, 1993.

4. See "Paul Chapman to Talk on Embattled Williamston," *Vineyard Gazette*, April 17, 1964; David Lillenthal Jr., "Williamston's Economic Future Is Bound to the Presence, or Absence, of Racial Troubles," *Vineyard Gazette*, August 11, 1964.

5. Milton Mazer, interview with Linsey Lee, Martha's Vineyard Museum Oral History Center, November 11, 1993.

6. Julia Rappaport, "Island to Honor Unlikely Ladies' Fight for Rights," *Vineyard Gazette*, September 21, 2007.

7. See Nancy Whiting, interview by Linsey Lee, Martha's Vineyard Museum Oral History Center, Nov. 15, 1993; "Five Women Take Food and Morale for Williamston," *Vineyard Gazette*, May 1, 1964.

8. "Bill of Rights? But This Is Williamston and We Have Rules Here, Policeman Said," *Vineyard Gazette*, May 8, 1964.

9. See Virginia Mazar, interview by Linsey Lee, Martha's Vineyard Museum Oral History Center, Nov. 11, 1993; Nancy Smith, interview by Linsey Lee, Martha's Vineyard Museum Oral History Center, Nov. 14, 1993; Nancy Whiting, interview by Linsey Lee, Martha's Vineyard Museum Oral History Center, Nov. 15, 1993; Peg Lilienthal, interview by Linsey Lee, Martha's Vineyard Museum Oral History Center, Nov. 26, 1993.

10. See "Bill of Rights? But This Is Williamston and We Have Rules Here, Policeman Said," *Vineyard Gazette*, May 8, 1964; Julia Wells, "Nancy Whiting Dies at Age 82; Was an Activist in Civil Causes," *Vineyard Gazette*, Sept. 25, 2007.

11. See Peg Lilienthal, interview by Linsey Lee, Martha's Vineyard Museum Oral History Center, Nov. 26, 1993; Virginia Mazer, interview by Linsey Lee, Martha's Vineyard Museum Oral History Center, Nov. 11, 1993.

12. W.H. Scarborough, "Williamston and the Silence of the Whites," *The Chapel Hill Weekly*, Aug. 26, 1964.

13. George Lawson to David King, "Report from Williamston," June 1, 1964, David King Papers, Duke University Library.

14. David Lilienthal, Jr., "Agitators and Outsiders are Not Welcome by White People in Racially Tense Williamston," *Vineyard Gazette*, July 31, 1964.

15. See "Amherst Pastor Aids NC Test of Rights Laws," *Springfield Union*, July 7, 1964; W.H. Scarborough, "Segregated-est Town in the U.S.A.," *The Chapel Hill Weekly*, July 26, 1964.

16. Peg Lilienthal, interview by Linsey Lee, Martha's Vineyard Museum Oral History Center, Nov. 26, 1993.

17. W.H. Scarborough, "Segregated-est Town in the U.S.A.," *The Chapel Hill Weekly*, July 26, 1964.

18. See David E. Lilienthal, "Agitators and Outsiders Are Now Welcome by the White People in Racially Tense Williamston," *Vineyard Gazette*, July 31, 1964. W.H. Scarborough, "Williamston and the Press," *The Chapel Hill Weekly*, August 12, 1964.

19. Susan Olzak and Emily Ryo, "Organizational Diversity, Vitality and Outcomes in the Civil Rights Movement," *Social Forces* 85, no. 4 (2007): 1590.

20. See W.H. Scarborough, "Williamston and the Press," *The Chapel Hill Weekly*, August 12, 1964. W.H. Scarborough, "Segregated-est Town in the U.S.A.," *The Chapel Hill Weekly*, July 26, 1964.

21. See W.H. Scarborough, "Williamston and the Press," *The Chapel Hill Weekly*, August 12, 1964. W.H. Scarborough, "Golden Frinks: The Sparkplug," *The Chapel Hill Weekly*, August 2, 1964.

22. Clarence Biggs, interview with author, October 6, 2005.

Chapter Nine

1. Richard Eugene Rogers, interview by author, Oct. 9, 2005.

2. Martin County Board of Education, Minutes, Book 5, 1959–1976, Williamston, NC, 108.

3. Marie Robertson, interview by author, Oct. 7, 2005.

4. See Ida Speller, reflection, July 30, 2011; Alma Purvis, interview by author, July 29, 2011; Jackie Bond, interview by author, Jan. 18, 2012. Styron Bond, Jr., interview by author, Mar. 1, 2008.

5. See Alton Hopewell, interview by author, June 22, 2005; Jawara K. Lumumba to author, May 2004.

6. Alma Purvis, interview by author, July 29, 2011.

7. See Brenda Whelchel, interview by author, Oct. 7, 2005; Alma Purvis, interview by author, July 29, 2011.

8. Alma Purvis, interview by author, July 29, 2011.

9. Martin County Board of Education, Minutes, Book 5, 1959–1976, Williamston, NC, 101.

10. See Golden Frinks, "NC Field Secretary Report," Southern Christian Leadership Conference Papers, Feb. 10–17, 1964; Golden Frinks, "Political Action Campaign Report," Southern Christian Leadership Conference Papers, Mar. 20, 1964; John Gibson, "Report Voter Registration in Eastern North Carolina," Southern Christian Leadership Conference Papers, Aug. 24, 1964; Edwina Smith, "Report to Reverend LaGarde," Southern Christian Leadership Conference Papers, June 2, 1964; Lois Harris Greene to author, "Memories of the Williamston Movement," July 20, 2011; Earl Newsome, interview by author, Dec. 28, 2012.

11. Martin County Board of Education, Minutes, Book 5, 1959–1976, Williamston, NC, 112.

12. Martin County Board of Education, Minutes, Book 5, 1959–1976, Williamston, NC, 129.

13. Richard Eugene Rogers, interview by author, Oct. 9, 2005.

14. See Marie Robertson, interview by author, Oct. 7, 2005; Clarence Biggs, interview by author, Oct. 6, 2005.

15. See Martin County Board of Education, Minutes, Book 5, 1959–1976, Williamston, NC, 147–170; Martin County Board of Education, Minutes, Book 5, 1959–1976, Williamston, NC, 4.

16. See Haul Reddick, interview by author, Mar. 27, 2008; Richard Eugene Rogers, interview by author, Oct. 9, 2005.

17. William Earl Newsome, interview by author, Dec. 28, 2012; "Negro Citizens In Contests for Two Boards-Register," *The Enterprise*, Mar. 21, 1968; "Four Contests on County Ballot In May 4th Primary," *The Enterprise*, Mar. 26, 1968.

18. See Alton Hopewell, interview by author, June 22, 2005; Jawara K. Lumumba to author, May 2004.

19. See "Limited Boycott Reported in County Schools Today," *The Enterprise*, Aug. 27, 1968; Clarence Biggs, interview by author, Oct. 6, 2005; David Cecelski, *Along Freedom Road: Hyde County, North Carolina, and the Fate of Black Schools in the South* (Chapel Hill: University of North Carolina Press, 1994), 68; "Normal Attendance Reported at School," *The Enterprise*, Sept. 3, 1963.

20. See "Around \$712,000 in School Funds Hit by Cut-Off Order," *The Enterprise*, Feb. 6, 1969; "Education Board in Huddle with Team from HEW," *The Enterprise*, Feb. 4, 1969; "Team from HEW Expresses Belief a Plan Will Evolve," *The Enterprise*, Feb. 6, 1969; Martin County Board of Education, Minutes, Book 5, 1959–1976, Williamston, NC, 55; "School Plans Still Not in Final Form as Talks Continue," *The Enterprise*, Feb. 18, 1969; Marie Robertson, interview by author, Oct. 7, 2005.

21. See "Total Integration Promised for the Term In 1970–71," *The Enterprise*, Mar. 4, 1969; "School Board to Proceed with its Plans for School," *The Enterprise*, Mar. 4, 1969; Alton Hopewell, interview by author, June 22, 2005; Richard Eugene Rogers, interview by author, Oct. 9, 2005.

22. See Charles Bullock and Harrell Rogers, "Coercion to Compliance: Southern School Districts and School Desegregation Guidelines," *The Journal of Politics* 38 (Nov. 1976): 1000–1002; Richard Eugene Rogers, interview by author, Oct. 9, 2005.

Chapter Ten

1. Styron Bond, Jr., interview by author, Mar. 1, 2008; Herman Boone, interview by author, October 14, 2012.

2. See Alton Hopewell, interview by author, June 22, 2005; Willis Williams, interview by author, June 8, 2011; Richard

Eugene Rogers, interview by author, Oct. 9, 2005.

3. See Dr. Richard Mizelle to author, May 27, 2013; "A Survey of NC Rosenwald's Schools," NC State Historical Preservation Office Department of Cultural Resources, accessed May 28, 2013, http://www.hpo.ncdcr.gov/rosenwald/rosenwald.htm.

Bibliography

Oral Histories

Biggs, Clarence, black teacher. Interview by author. Williamston, NC, Oct. 6, 2005.

Bond, Jackie, black activist. Interview by author. Jan. 18, 2012.

Bond, Styron, Jr., black activist. Interview by author. Williamston, NC, Mar. 1, 2008.

Boone, Herman, black teacher and coach. Interview by author, Oct. 14, 2012.

Bryd, Reverend Henry, white minister and activist. Interview by Linsey Lee, Martha's Vineyard Museum Oral History Center, Nov. 25, 1993.

Chapman, Rev. Paul, white minister and activist. Interview by Linsey Lee, Martha's Vineyard Museum Oral History Center, Sept. 26, 2008.

Conway, Betsy, white student. Interview by author. Williamston, NC, July 17, 2011.

Conway, Bob, white student. Interview by author. Williamston, NC, July 17, 2011.

Corey, George, white businessman and member of town council. Interview by author. Williamston, NC, July 17, 2011.

Greene, Lois, black activist. Interview by author. Williamston, NC, Nov. 10, 2012.

___. "Memories of the Williamston Movement," correspondence, July 20, 2011.

Hargett, Ralph, black activist. Interview by author. Oct. 29, 2012.

Hopewell, Alton, white teacher. Interview by author. Williamston, NC, June 22, 2005.

King, Francis, black activist. Interview by author. Williamston, NC, Oct. 22, 2005.

Lilienthal, Peg, white activist. Interview by Linsey Lee, Martha's Vineyard Museum Oral History Center, Nov. 26, 1993.

Lumumba, Jawara K., black student. Personal correspondence with author, May 2004.

Marshall, Ollie, black activist and daughter of Mary Mobley. Interview by author. July 9, 2011.

Mazer, Milton, husband of white activist Virginia Mazer. Interview by Linsey Lee, Martha's Vineyard Museum Oral History Center, Nov. 11, 1993.

Mazer, Virginia, white activist. Interview by Linsey Lee, Martha's Vineyard Museum Oral History Center, Nov. 11, 1993.

Murphy, Polly, white activist. Interview by Linsey Lee, Martha's Vineyard Museum Oral History Center, Nov. 7, 1993.

Newsome, William Earl, black activist. Interview by author. Williamston, NC, Dec. 28, 2012.

Purvis, Alma, black activist. Interview by author. Greensboro, NC, July 29, 2011.

Purvis, Bob, black activist. Interview by author. Greensboro, NC, July 29, 2011.

Reddick, Haul, white businessman. Interview by author. Williamston, NC, Mar. 27, 2008.

Robertson, Marie, white teacher. Interview by author. Williamston, NC, Oct. 7, 2005.

Rogers, Richard Eugene, white superintendent. Interview by author. Williamston, NC, Oct. 9, 2005.

Smith, Nancy, white activist. Interview by Linsey Lee, Martha's Vineyard Museum Oral History Center, Nov. 14, 1993.

Speller, Ida Small, black activist and daughter of Sarah Small. Interview by author. July 13, 2011.

___. Reflection written by Speller, July 30, 2011.

Spruill, Ruth, black student and daughter of Mary Mobley. Interview by author. July 9, 2011.

Thigpen, Joseph, white county commissioner. Interview by author. Williamston, NC, April 12, 2008.

Whelchel, Brenda, white student. Interview by author. Williamston, NC, Oct. 7, 2005.

Whiting, Nancy, white activist. Interview by Linsey Lee, Martha's Vineyard Museum Oral History Center, Nov. 15, 1993.

Williams, Willis, black activist. Interview by author. Jamesville, NC, June 8, 2011.

Video

Small, Booker, and Ida Small Speller. *Sarah Small's Freedom Fighters Legacy.* Film. Directed by Booker Small. Boston: Longshots Videographer, 2011.

Public Records

Martin County Board of Education, 1963–1970.

Martin County Court Records, 1957–1970.

North Carolina Mayors Co-operating Committee. *North Carolina and the Negro,* 1964.

U.S. Bureau of the Census, 1960.

Papers

David King Papers, Duke University

Southern Christian Leadership Conference Papers, Emory University

Newspapers

The Chapel Hill Weekly
Charlotte News
The (Greenville, NC) *Daily Reflector*
The (Williamston, NC) *Enterprise*
Herford County (Ahoskie, NC) *Herald*
Journal and Guide (Norfolk, VA)
Martha's Vineyard Gazette
The (Raleigh, NC) *News and Observer*
The (Lumberton, NC) *Robesonian*
Springfield (MA) *Union*
The (Norfolk, VA) *Virginian-Pilot*
Washington (NC) *Daily News*

Theses

Watson, Chelsea R. "A Historical Analysis of the Civil Rights Movement in Windsor, Bertie County, North Carolina, 1963–1968." Master's thesis, Morgan State University, Dec. 2007.

Articles

Bullock, Charles, and Harrell Rogers. "Coercion to Compliance: Southern School Districts and School Desegregation Guidelines." *The Journal of Politics* 38 (Nov. 1976): 987–1011.

Calvino, Manuel. "Reflections on Community Studies." *Journal of Community Psychology* 26, no. 3 (May 1998): 253–259.

Carter, David. "The Williamston Freedom Movement: Civil Rights at the Grass Roots in Eastern North Carolina, 1957–1964." *The North Carolina*

Historical Review 126, no. 1 (Jan. 1999): 1–42.

Critcher, III, Allen. "Local Civil Rights Leader Recalls the Movement." *The Enterprise Centennial Edition*, Sept. 1999.

Harris, Nelson. "The Implementation of the Desegregation Decision in North Carolina." *The Journal of Negro History* 34, no. 3 (Summer 1955): 310–317.

Mitchell, Francis. "Did N.C. Whites Kill A&T Student by Mistake?" *Jet* 13, no. 2, Nov. 14, 1957, 48–52.

Olzak, Susan, and Emily Ryo. "Organizational Diversity, Vitality and Outcomes in the Civil Rights Movement." *Social Forces* 85, no. 4 (2007): 1590.

Vanfossen, Beth. "Variables Related to Resistance to Desegregation in the South." *Social Forces* 47, no. 1 (1968): 39–44.

Books

Cecelski, David. *Along Freedom Road: Hyde County, North Carolina, and the Fate of Black Schools in the South.* Chapel Hill: University of North Carolina Press, 1994.

Chapman, Rev. Paul. Autobiography. 2000.

Daniels, Pete. *The Lost Social Revolution: The South in the 1950s.* Chapel Hill: University of North Carolina Press, 2000.

Fairclough, Adam. *To Redeem the Soul of America: The Southern Christian Leadership Conference and Martin Luther King, Jr.* Athens: University of Georgia Press, 1987.

Garrow, David. *Bearing the Cross: Martin Luther King, Jr., and the Southern Christian Leadership Conference.* New York: Perennial Classics, 1999.

Johnson, Suzan, ed. *Wise Women Bearing Gifts.* Valley Forge, PA: Judson Press, 1988.

Wells, Goldie Frinks, and Crystal Sanders. *Golden Asro Frinks: Telling the Unsung Song.* Salt Lake City: Aardvark Global, 2009.